Graham

Graham

Graham Hill with Neil Ewart

St. Martin's Press

Library of Congress Cataloging in Publication Data

Hill, Graham, 1929-1975.
  Graham Hill.

  1. Hill, Graham, 1929-1975. 2. Automobile racing
drivers—Great Britain—Biography. I. Ewart, Neil.
II. Title.
GV1032.H48A34   796.7'2'0924 [B]   77-72299
ISBN 0-312-34212-8

Contents

Foreword

by HRH the Prince of Wales

I was surprised and honoured when I received an invitation to write the foreword to this book and I found myself accepting without hesitation. From the first moment that I met Graham Hill I became a devoted admirer and it was always the greatest possible fun to meet him on the various occasions that our paths crossed. To me he was the embodiment of all the best that is implied by the word 'fun'. His zest for life was intoxicating and with it went a memorable sense of humour, which never failed to appeal to all ages.

Several years ago when an uncle of mine died, to whom I was devoted, I remember being distraught at the misery of the whole thing until his widow told me she was sure he would far rather I remembered the fun and happiness we had had instead of being too sad. I shall always remember the fun and happiness of those occasions when I saw Graham. He took me driving twice – once round Brands Hatch and once round Thruxton. On both occasions he showed me how to get the best out of my Aston Martin, but I remember becoming rather uneasy as we screeched round the track with Graham at the wheel, clouds of blue smoke pouring from the tyres and fearful squeaking noises coming from the suspension. I kept trying to remind him that I *had* intended to keep my car for as many years as possible, but I don't think he heard

7

me! The Thruxton occasion was more memorable because, contrary to what Graham says in Chapter 10, I *did* spin off the track and ended up on the grass in a rather dizzy condition, everything having happened far too quickly to be frightened. I remember flashing past the pits and seeing everyone waving at me through the drizzle, only to realize from Graham's ashen face shortly afterwards that they were in fact trying to tell me to slow down!

His courage and determination were legendary. I shall never forget the sight of him strapped to a revolving typist's chair in the back of an open land-rover (only shortly after his release from hospital) and bearing an extraordinary resemblance to a human form of Gatling Gun as he loosed off at some unsuspecting pheasant. By his determination to get back to motor racing he was an outstanding example and inspiration to thousands of people – not to mention the inspiration he was to young, old and disabled in so many walks of life. He was also an inspiration to his family. You only have to read Bette Hill's incredibly moving chapter at the end of the book to see that. It brought a very large lump to my throat to read what she said, but it also showed what a courageous and unique person Graham had married and what a source of strength they must both have been to each other.

This book is immensely enjoyable to read and contains many aspects of Graham's profound and refreshing philosophy on life, which we could all do well to ponder over from time to time. But above all, reading this book makes you realize just what a loss we have all suffered by Graham's departure. I, for one, am deeply grateful that I had the chance to know him and there will be countless thousands like myself who will always remember his extraordinary qualities, which inspired such affection and devotion wherever he went.

Publishers' Note

The publishers are glad to acknowledge the help of Graham Hill's autobiography, *Life At the Limit*, in the preparation of *Graham*. *Life At the Limit* is a full account of Graham Hill's racing experience up to 1969, published by William Kimber.

Acknowledgements

Permission to use copyright photographs is acknowledged as follows: Syndication International 1, 4, 13, 14, 28, 35, 36, 37; Phipps Photographic 3; *Coventry Evening Telegraph* 5; *Kent Messenger* 7: Popperfoto 8, 9; London Express Pictures 10, 15, 30, 34; Rex Features 11; David James 16; ATV Network 32, 39; *Hackney Gazette* 41, 42; Victor Blackman 43; Michael Alcott 44; Michael Turner 23, 24, 25, 26; Sqd. Ldr David Checketts 17; C. White 18; Franco Lini 20; Sheridan Coakley 29; Scope Features 22; Arthur G. Gibson 19; Associated Newspapers 2, 31, 38; Keystone Press Agency 33, 40.

I

The Boy Least Likely

It's appropriate, I suppose, that my entry into this world was a race. With both their wives pregnant at the same time, and in the same nursing home in Hampstead, my father and his brother had a wager on, as to which would be the first to have a son. That was one race I didn't win; they both produced sons at identical times, and so it was a dead heat.

When I was a young boy one of my early toys was a mechanical one, a Meccano set. I used to visit a second-hand shop nearby and buy bits that were nothing to do with the actual Meccano and add to it at intervals. When I say buy, that's rather grand, I'd usually got tuppence and that was a lot of money in those days, so I left a deposit and saved up for the rest. As I acquired each new part, so my father tells me, I'd often spend six or seven hours with my head between my knees working things out and fixing them into my Meccano set. Then, at the end of the day, I'd complain to my mother that I had a headache. The mechanical interest was obviously there early on and I was also a great bookworm.

Neither of these things was of much use to me when I went to a technical college later in Hendon. One of my classmates was a chap named Harry Hyams and he and I were picked out by the headmaster as the two boys least likely to succeed. I think the headmaster was half right. You've probably heard of Harry Hyams – he's the property developer and also a power-boat racer. He's done well – makes me feel quite a failure!

I left the college when I was sixteen and went to Smiths, the instrument makers. Although my father's business was on the Stock Exchange, he thought I had a mechanical bent. My father, by the way, is the most unmechanical man I've ever met and he's never driven a car in his life. My mother, on the other hand, owned a motor-cycle when she was seventeen. Anyway, I joined Smiths and served a five-year apprenticeship with them which gave me an extremely good grounding in engineering. I think my father rather hoped I'd end up as a captain of industry.

When Smiths sent me to their engineering college near Cheltenham for the final four years of the apprenticeship it posed a bit of a problem. I had a girl friend in London and the only way I could get to see her at weekends was by push-bike. London was 100 miles away and I used to cycle up every week-end to see her. As you can imagine, when I got there, I needn't have bothered. Try 100 miles on a bike and you'll see what I mean. I'd arrive on Saturday evening and then go back the 100 miles to Cheltenham again on Sunday afternoon – and that was the week-end. It was ridiculous.

There had to be a way of solving the problem and I saved up for a motor-bike, hoping this would get me there quicker and in better condition. It didn't work out that way – the bloody thing used to break down and I spent more time mending the motor-bike than I did getting up to London. Perhaps I should have stuck to the push-bike, for the motor-bike left a big impression on me . . . for life.

It did this when I was travelling across the Cotswold Hills one night in low cloud and mist. You know how it is. Some idiot had stopped his car with failed lights and I plunged straight into the back of it. When I left hospital after several months, my smashed left leg was half an inch shorter than the other one and it's remained that way, as well as bandy, ever since.

At twenty-one I was called up for two years' National Service. I went into the Navy as an ERA which, as you know, is an Engine Room Artificer – and as you will also know, is an Engineer. We were given the rank of Petty

Officer and eventually, I was given a ship. I wasn't actually given it – I was put in one. It was a 10000-ton cruiser HMS *Swiftsure* which was commissioned just before the war ended. I enjoyed it when I was given a propeller to look after. Fortunately there were three others on the ship (propellers – that is).

I was down in the engine-room in charge of the throttles which operated the steam turbines. It's quite difficult to get 10000 tons alongside a jetty but we had a Captain who was pretty good at it. He used to do it in about eight movements, but then we had a new Captain and he took eighty-eight movements to get alongside. I used to spend an hour leaping from one throttle to the other and I was absolutely whacked at the end of it. We'd all know when we were alongside: there'd be an enormous great clump and everyone in the engine-room would fall over. We went to the Mediterranean on courtesy trips – to Monte Carlo, San Remo, and Tangiers and I saw some interesting things there, of course, which I've never seen since. I've got quite a few things to thank the Navy for.

It was 1951 when we went to Monte Carlo and at the time I had absolutely no idea that they raced there. I just wandered around the place and won a few bob at the Casino. I never dreamt I'd be driving a racing car round that circuit in a Grand Prix one day. At that particular time I'd never even driven a car and I certainly had no ambitions of becoming a racing driver. I didn't even know that motor racing existed.

I was twenty-four before I first drove a car, which I bought from a friend of mine – at least, I thought he was a friend. It was a twenty-year-old Morris Eight with a canvas roof and I gave £110 for it. It was a real old heap. I managed to drive it back across London to my home. Then a few days later I got hold of some L-plates, fitted them, and went down and passed the driving test.

I hadn't owned the car long when a chap in a laundry van came out of a side turning and thumped me and wrote the car off.

That was shortly after I'd left the Navy and returned

to Smiths so, as I was without a car for recreation, I concentrated on my rowing. I'd been rowing for several years and still continued it when I was in the Navy. In fact, I met Bette at a rowing club when I was in the Navy – rowing for the Auriol Rowing Club at Hammersmith. It was a Boxing Day regatta and she'd come along with a girl friend who had become engaged to one of my crew members. When I was introduced to Bette I was told she'd been in the Wrens. This should have given us something in common right away but she told me some time afterwards that she wasn't impressed with me at all during that initial meeting. To her, I was just one of the fellows who was around. I put on my Petty Officer's uniform that night for the engagement party – and that was the begining of that. It just fell into place and we became regular boy and girl friend for the next five years, though our meetings were pretty spasmodic.

Bette took up rowing shortly after she met me. She rowed for the Stuart Ladies Rowing Club further along the Thames on the river Lea. There were only eight girls and a cox – just enough to make up one crew. They trained hard every night of the week as well as week-ends, like machines, and were really dedicated. Before long they had entered for the Head of the River race from Hammersmith to Mortlake. They only had an old clinker boat, which was heavier and slower in the water than the smooth shell boats, and yet they beat everyone and went 'Head' of the river.

The following year they managed to get a shell boat and they went Head of the River again – and in the year after that. I was really chuffed. When they decided to enter for the European Games I was even more pleased. I was their coach and they were to be the first British crew, male or female, to go to an international event. I rode along the tow-path on a bicycle to follow their progress on the river. Most rowing coaches did this – but I not only used the cycle as a form of transport to keep up with them, I also used it as a method of teaching them how to propel their boat more effectively. I'd get off, lift the front of the bike up, and gently tap the wheel – with each tap representing a stroke of their oars. If I tapped the wheel too softly it slowed – if I did so too hard it upset the rhythm, whereas regular and steady taps kept the wheel going smoothly round and round in a perfectly balanced rhythm.

The demonstration helped them get their boat going and when they went to the European Games – they won! The other crews – the Dutch, Russian, Czech, French and German girls – were all bigger and tougher and yet the British crew won the Games. It was fantastic.

You can't play at rowing, you have to be dedicated. You've got to concentrate, too, and these and many other things which I learnt when I was rowing helped me when I became a racing driver. I thoroughly enjoyed rowing and I was very proud to have stroked the London Rowing Club first eight in the Grand Challenge Cup at Henley. I've continued to be a member of the club and that's why I have carried the club's dark blue and white colours on my helmet ever since I took up motor racing. These were the only two sports I was really any good at. Both sitting down sports, you'll notice, and I was even facing the wrong way in one of them.

When I had finished rowing for the season, after I'd returned to Smiths, I saw a magazine advertisement which said that anyone interested could drive a racing car at Brands Hatch for five shillings a lap. I went down and did four laps. It was the most important pound I ever spent. Up to that stage I never really knew what I was going to do in life. I knew I was an engineer and that I was working with Smiths, but the moment I did those four laps everything changed.

The sensation of power and speed fascinated me and so did the knowledge that if I wanted I could develop more and more power and still control it. After those laps my next thought was how to get back in the car again without paying.

The racing school at Brands Hatch was called the Universal Motor Racing Club. It was the only school in

existence at that time as far as I know. I hadn't any
money so I approached the owner and asked him if I
could work on his car as a mechanic in return for letting
me drive it by way of payment. He agreed but, unfortunately, he wasn't a businessman and he made a bit
of a pig's ear of the whole thing. One day when I arrived
the car had disappeared. He'd bought it on hire purchase,
apparently, and must have defaulted on payments because
the snatch-back men had come along and taken the car
away. He disappeared too and I never saw him again. I'd
been helping him in the evenings and during week-ends
and was left high and dry with my motor racing career
cut short before it had even started.

Shortly afterwards I was in a pub in Paddington
round about Christmas and met another fellow who
wanted to start a racing drivers' school. I told him I was
just the bloke he was looking for. He bought a couple of
Formula 3 cars and I ended up working on them full-time
at Westerham in Kent. As you can imagine, I had to
leave Smiths – otherwise I couldn't have worked on the
cars. I still hadn't any money, and he wasn't going to pay
me, so I jacked it in at Smiths and went on the dole. I
used to go to the Labour Exchange every Wednesday and
Friday morning to collect 32s. 6d. a week – I gather it's a
bit more now – but that just about paid for the fare to
Westerham every day so I could work on the racing cars.

The arrangement this time wasn't just to be allowed to
drive one of the cars, in return for my work, but actually
to drive one in a race. I really worked hard at stripping
the cars down. My mother knew I had left Smiths and
she fed and housed me and kept the secret; but my
father thought I was still gainfully employed at Smiths
because I used to disappear from home at the crack of
dawn and come back late at night.

I carried on like this for about three months and then
the owner of the cars kept his word and let me enter for a
race at Brands Hatch. That was in April 1954. We had
only one member in the club and that was me so the

choice of driver was pretty clear cut. I'd never been to a motor race and I'd only been driving an ordinary car for a year. My only experience of driving a racing car was during those four laps at Brands Hatch. So the first race I saw was the one I was in. It was a very small race and not very important but I managed to come second in the heat and fourth in the final.

The Labour Exchange soon began to get a bit stroppy about handing out the 32s. 6d. to me each week. When I'd signed on I had told them that I wanted a job as a racing driver. They hadn't got any jobs for racing drivers but they had written it down, and now started sending me along to all kinds of other jobs. I made sure I couldn't do them so, after four months, they had to drum me out of the club for not trying.

The car owner had been delighted with the race and had gone flat out on advertising the school, which he called the Premier Motor Racing Club. I was still the mechanic, and the only member, when six other chaps joined.

As money was coming in now I felt I ought to get some of it. I was finding it difficult to get to Westerham now that the dole money had dried up. I wasn't eating much either, and I was getting a bit thin. So I asked for £3 a week. It would just about cover the bus fares and leave a bit over for nosh.

I stayed on to help get the club going. On our first day, all six members turned up with their gear. As I was the only one who had raced I was the obvious choice for instructor. I worked on the two cars round the back, took off my overalls, drove the transport to the track – and then put on a white coat and set about turning them into Grand Prix stars. It took a bit of doing as they were scared stiff.

I decided to do one more race with the club before we finally parted company. I didn't get far because something in the engine broke after I'd done exactly one lap and that was the end of that.

All I could do now was watch, so I stayed on at Brands.

While I was there I got talking to one or two people and as one of them had a transporter I asked him if he could give me a lift back to London. He said: 'Yes, certainly,' so I went back with him – and his name was Colin Chapman.

When we got back to the stable in Hornsey which was the Lotus works – in those days producing one car a week – I noticed there was only one man and a boy available to repair their rather bent-looking Lotus in time for the next race meeting. So I suggested I gave a hand. Colin said okay and paid me a pound a day which, of course, was considerably more than I *hadn't* been getting.

I worked on the racing car in the evenings and on the production car during the day and on other people's cars at week-ends. In this way I got to know quite a few people. I also made one or two contacts at the Steering Wheel Club in Mayfair. I wasn't a member but I gave everyone the impression I was.

My intention was to offer my services again in return for drives but there weren't all that number of people who were sufficiently hard up for a mechanic to let them drive their precious racers. But I did meet Danny Margulies and he accepted me as his unpaid mechanic. We went on a tour of Europe together, he racing a C-Type Jaguar and I preparing it. The car was so reliable, though, that there wasn't much for me to do to it, but it was quite an experience. We used to sleep rough in the transport-truck beside the road, or in haystacks.

I still wasn't getting into racing as a driver in the way that I wished but I did go along with him as a rider-mechanic during a race in Sardinia in which we finished third overall.

Later in the summer we drove the truck from London to Sicily. The journey took six days but it was worth it because I was to have my first real chance at actually driving in a race in which the top drivers of the day were taking part – including Mike Hawthorn. It was to be a ten-hour night race around the streets of Messina with me as Danny's co-driver. I'd never driven in a race at night and when my stint came to take over I screeched around the town determined to out-drive all the aces and really put myself on the map. It sent the old adrenalin surging but then Danny spun during one of his stints at the wheel and ruptured the fuel tank and we had to pack it in.

I had to get back to London in a hurry as Bette and I were due to be married the following Saturday. If I travelled back in the truck it would take six days, so I elected to go by train which took forty-eight hours.

When the wedding day arrived I had precisely 1s. 6d. in the bank and £5 in my pocket. Bette provided £12 from her earnings as a secretary to pay for the reception, and a friend lent me a twenty-year-old banger for our brief honeymoon in Bognor.

We stayed in the grottiest room in the worst hotel to make my fiver last – but even then we could only manage one week-end. I had suggested Bognor for our honeymoon as it was close to the Goodwood circuit where there was a race on. I was to be reserve driver for Team Lotus and that was the sort of offer I couldn't afford to pass up – even on our honeymoon. It was to be a nine-hour race but, like so many understudies in the theatre, I was never called on to the stage as the principal star. Keith Hall gave the main performance and I had to be content with two laps during practice – at night.

After that it did occur to me that I ought to start supporting my wife and myself, so I started to work full-time at Lotus who were pretty big in the racing car production business by then. Two years had passed since I'd done those initial five-bob laps at Brands Hatch and I still wasn't getting any nearer to my goal of becoming a racing driver as Lotus required me as an engineer – but it did bring in £9 a week.

We got a little flat in London. We had to climb over the bicycles in the hall to get to it and share the bathroom with nine other people – but not all at once, thank goodness. The rent was five guineas a week and it didn't leave much of my wages, so Bette had to go on working. We couldn't afford to start a family; even clothes were a luxury. We've never regretted the tough times – they strengthened our marriage and knocked off any starry illusions.

2

Early Days

I have to thank Colin Chapman for putting me on the track as a driver. He let me use a car I had worked on while I was a full-time engineer at Lotus, and I entered it for the 1956 *Autosport* Championship series. It had only a 40 b.h.p. engine, so it wasn't exactly overpowered; but it was quite good and I used to climb into it with Bette and drive to the circuits – then take the hood off, slip the numbers on and race it.

I did quite well and arrived at the situation where, if I won the final event at Oulton Park, I stood to become champion. I took the engine down and did a real tweak-up job on it – but it blew up during the race and I lost the Championship. No one was to blame but me because I'd over-tightened a con-rod bolt and it just snapped.

Colin Chapman signed me up to drive for Team Lotus in 1957 and the following year, and so it came about that I had my first Grand Prix in 1958. That was at Monte Carlo and it was Lotus's first Grand Prix as well. It's a very tight circuit round the streets and at that time only sixteen starters were allowed. They used to invite about twenty-four cars and there was a terrific scrabble to qualify for the race.

Bette had never been to Monte Carlo so I drove her down in an Austin A35 which I had acquired and we made it in pretty good time. When we arrived we heard that the transporter, carrying my Lotus and that of my team-mate Cliff Allison, had broken down. Colin Chapman's wife, Hazel, and Cliff's wife, Mabel, had come along, so Bette had company and it was like a holiday for the three girls. But for Cliff and me things were getting a bit desperate.

The transporter only just made it in time and we were the last two to qualify. The race was a hundred laps in those days. I qualified for the sixteenth spot which meant that at the start of the race I was last; by the seventy-fifth lap, I found myself in fourth place.

It all seemed too easy but then, as I went down to the sea front and was turning right, the revs suddenly shot up and I spun round. I thought: 'Bloody hell – it's jumped out of gear.' I looked in the cockpit and started to wham it through the gears . . . brrrm, brrrm, and all that stuff and nothing happened – then I looked up and saw that my back wheel had fallen off.

When I got out I fell over. I was suffering from heat exhaustion and didn't know it. In those days we had the engine in the front of the car and all the heat from it and the exhaust pipes came back through the cockpit. We used to get burns on our feet and legs, too. It was impossible to seal the bulkhead and drivers got dehydrated. Heat exhaustion can be very dangerous because one is not aware of its build-up and eventually you could be changing up instead of down, miss your braking point, and be going round in a bit of a haze. We don't have these problems now because the engines are behind us. Even the radiators are at the back, so there's no heat at all. We also have the monocoque construction, which is a sort of aluminium tub that we sit in, and it's completely sealed.

Having dropped out of my first Grand Prix through a wheel falling off it seemed logical to try to make up for the disappointment with another wheel, at the Casino that night. I couldn't go wrong. I won time and time again and scooped £120. Bette went through some nail-biting moments as I kept doubling up, and I was still winning when she and Jack Brabham and a few others pulled me away from the table.

I was also racing Formula 2 and sports cars for Lotus

that year and in one race at Silverstone I was completing the last lap, in the lead, when my brakes went at 120 m.p.h. The brake fluid had leaked away and I was a bit worried about what would happen next. At times like these it's essential to do *something*. By figuring it out, and acting, it takes your mind off being frightened.

Roy Salvadori and Keith Hall were catching me so fast they were bound to overtake me. In the last corner I went in much, much faster then they did, only because I had no brakes and couldn't stop. The desperate slide through the corner and over the finishing line that followed gave me the race.

I also enjoyed driving saloon cars as they provided a bit of light relief. I entered one race at Brands Hatch in which Les Leston was taking part. I'll never forget his comments to an interviewer later. He said: 'I was driving a Riley 1·5 and some little bugger in a green and yellow A35 had the audacity to beat me. That was Graham Hill – and I was saloon car champion at the time!' When I introduced myself in the paddock and asked him what he thought of the A35 he just said: 'Oh, that was quite good, sonny. Run along.' We became good friends later, despite that unpromising beginning.

It was around that time that I formed a company called Speedwell Conversions, with three other friends, which made bolt-on goodies for Minis and other cars. So I entered a Mini for one of the saloon car races at Brands. The 3·8 Jaguars were hot favourites and kings of the track, so we added some nitro-methane to our fuel. It was against the regulations, of course, and you've got to watch it otherwise it can cause an explosion. It's lethal stuff but it really gives the engine some stick.

When we got the Mini on the line for the race I didn't start up because I knew that the officials would probably start choking and gasping for breath and someone might twig. The nitro takes all the oxygen out of the air, and if you get round the exhaust you can't breathe; your eyes run and it's really terrible.

So I started the engine at the last moment and when the

flag dropped I went off like a fart in a hurricane – weaving in and out among the Jaguars and overtaking one or two of them. It was a helluva hoot while it lasted but then my engine blew up. Incidentally, don't ever try nitro-methane. It really is lethal; I must have been mad to use it, and I never did so again.

I didn't do very well in Formula 1 racing that year. I won my first two World Championship points in the Italian Grand Prix at Monza but that was the limit of my success. The race was full of incidents including brake failure early on, three stops to top up the water in a split radiator and later on – a small fire for good measure. That extinguished itself but I ran out of fuel on the last lap and coasted over the line into fifth place – out of fuel, out of water and out of brakes.

In the French Grand Prix at Rheims I took one 160 m.p.h. corner half standing in the cockpit. The crowd thought I had gone mad – but the gearbox had got so hot it melted the solder holding the oil-filler cap in place and boiling oil was splashing over my legs.

That race was the great forty-seven-year-old Fangio's last before he retired. He held five world titles in only seven years' championship racing, and had won twenty-four Grands Prix. He was one of the greatest drivers of all time – probably *the* greatest, and I felt honoured to have been in the same race. He's the most impressive man I've ever met. He still went to the circuits after he retired and if you were there and heard the crowd cheering suddenly for no apparent reason, you knew Fangio had arrived. He was the maestro and they loved him. Whenever he entered a room everyone sensed his presence even before they turned round and set eyes on him. The championship points that he accumulated in 51 races over those seven active years of racing were to take me 116 races and eleven years to match – before I became the first driver to beat his points record.

At this stage in my driving career I still had a long way to go before I really arrived on the scene. I was proud of those two points in my first year of Grand Prix racing.

I was even more proud of them the following year because I never scored any at all.

That was 1959, when I was still with Lotus and we didn't feature too well. After two seasons of Grand Prix racing I had finished once and only scored those two World Championship points. So I told Colin Chapman I was brassed-off and that I was going to join BRM for 1960. It was like jumping out of the frying-pan into the fire because, at that time, BRM hadn't had any luck either. Of course, directly I joined BRM, Lotus started winning – so there was a coincidence!

3
World Champion – First Time

The start of a race is the most thrilling moment in any sport. In motor racing the noise builds up, the tension builds up and there's nothing like it – to *watch* that is. Inside the car you're shut off, waiting for the flag to drop. You can't hear the engine because of the noise from the other cars. I never take my eyes off the starter after the one-minute signal. You can see the rev counter out of the corner of your eye and you've also got the vibration of the engine to help you – but you need three eyes: one for the flag, one on the rev counter and one looking for gaps in case the car in front stalls. This escape hole is vital. I've been banged quite a few times on the grid. At Brands Hatch, once, the bloke behind me got off to a flier and shunted me up the bank on the left. I'd only gone fifty yards and it was all over.

When you get into a racing car you put it on the way you put on a suit. Once you're wearing the car you begin to paint a picture with it. I like to compare the art of motor racing with that of an artist painting a picture; the circuit is the canvas and the car the brush and paint. Both artists use their brush to prove something. I used my brush, or car, in an attempt to prove I was the best driver and this made me put everything I'd got into winning. You can get some idea of an artist from the picture he or she has painted – and the sort of person you are also shows in the way you drive. I'm seldom satisfied with my performance because I'm seeking perfection all the time. If I have just won a race my next concern is to win the next. If I'm running a racing team, I want to help it do well and then do better.

When he takes part in a race, every driver puts his life in the hands of all the other drivers. He has to trust they won't make mistakes and jeopardize his safety. It's the same in ordinary driving when we go out on the roads. We all assume that the other drivers will keep to the correct side of the road and not start driving on the wrong side, that they'll stop at a red traffic light – that sort of thing. The same thing applies to motor racing but to a much higher degree. We have the advantage of all driving in the same direction (most of the time, anyway). But things can and do go wrong. It's a shocking thing to be in an accident yourself, or to see another. But, basically, I'm optimistic; we have to be in this business. Some people think that the main quality needed by a racing driver is courage. But you could say, and I believe this, that women are brave because having a baby takes courage. It's the same mixture of a lot of pain and a lot of pleasure.

Part of the enjoyment of motor racing for me is the people one meets. There's no question about doping or pulling races. It's a clean sport and I think all those involved in it are extremely pleasant people. The cars are pleasant, too – and so are the engines. They're like a piece of modern sculpture. They're beautifully designed and wonderfully made – and they work. Most sculptures don't work, but an engine does. It actually lives and breathes and it's quite something.

The aim in any race is to get into the lead and stay there. This isn't easy, of course, and the chances are that you'll lose it and several laps will pass before you can regain it. This is where racing tactics come in and I had one of my first tactical dices with Stirling Moss at the Dutch Grand Prix soon after I joined BRM in 1960. I really had to work out what was happening in that race and plan by driving realistically.

I was near the front of the pack towards the end of the race but Stirling was gaining on me. If I gave the BRM more stick I risked a break-down. So I tried to work out just how fast he was gaining. I reckoned it was two seconds a lap and with twelve laps to go my twenty-six seconds' lead should put me two seconds in front of Stirling at the finish. That was the theory – and it wasn't far out. I crossed the line a second and a half ahead of him. The fact that I had held my place and finished third ahead of Stirling did a great deal to boost my morale for the future.

Later on, in the British Grand Prix at Silverstone, I drove what was probably one of my best races, but I made a real monkey's of it at the start. I had done well in practice and got myself on the front row of the grid. But when the race started I stalled on the line. There was no excuse, I was just plain stupid. Tony Brooks was behind and it didn't do him much good but his car gave me a push-start and I was able to set off in chase of the others.

I gradually worked my way through the field and managed to overtake Jack Brabham, the leader, on the fifty-fifth lap and kept ahead of him by one or two seconds. Then I began to experience a little brake trouble and this presented a problem as I was approaching Copse Corner where, with only five laps to go, I came across two tail-enders immediately in my path. Jack was only a second behind me and putting on the pressure, so this left me with two choices. I could overtake the two cars and go into the corner before they did – or stay behind and follow them through. If I stayed behind I would lose time to Jack and run the risk of him passing me. If I overtook them I would arrive at the corner just that much faster and have to rely on faulty brakes.

I elected to go past them and, of course, the moment I arrived in the corner too fast the brakes didn't work – and I spun off and ended up in the ditch. I had made the wrong decision and paid for it. But on occasions like this there's only one thing to do – put the experience gained into the bank, as it were, to draw on in future races.

We bought a house at Mill Hill around this time. Things were looking up, and 1962 was to be the turning point for me. I was still with BRM and I notched up my first Formula 1 victory ever in the Easter meeting at Goodwood. This was the occasion when Stirling Moss had his tragic accident. Stirling had made a couple of pit-stops because of problems with his car and lost valuable time. He made a brilliant attempt to get back into the race and broke the course record in doing so. I was leading the race comfortably, with Stirling still two laps behind me – when he flew past on the outside of a bend. Normally Stirling would never have attempted to pass anyone there – and as he overtook me he was already off the track and on the grass and then, for no apparent reason, he just ploughed straight on into the bank.

The accident was horrific. It took half an hour to cut him out of the wreckage. His face was smashed, his left side paralysed, and he didn't regain consciousness for a month. When he did eventually come round in hospital he couldn't remember a thing – the race or the accident – nor even getting out of bed that morning and going to Goodwood, and it's remained that way ever since.

When he passed me he seemed to be completely out of control. Just what happened no one will ever know – but I'm absolutely sure it wasn't due to driver error.

Stirling recovered, as we all know, but the accident ended his racing career as a driver, and that is one of the saddest things that ever happened for the sport. Stirling was one of the greatest drivers the world has ever known. He always managed to give his best in any type of car, which made him an extremely versatile driver, and he never seemed to have an off-day.

I've been involved in several accidents and I've seen many others. I've also seen drivers killed and lost many personal friends. Jimmy Clark, for instance, who was one of the greatest racers of all time. Jo Bonnier, Bruce McLaren, Piers Courage, Jochen Rindt, Jo Siffert, François

Cevert, Peter Revson. All of them killed and one could include many more names – but what's the point? They died doing what they enjoyed most.

What do we do – prohibit racing? If people like go-karting, in my opinion, they should go go-karting. If they like motor rallying they should go rallying, and if they like motor racing they should go racing. I'm for all of them. How is anyone going to stop people losing their lives? From the humanitarian point of view it does come in – but who is going to turn round and say, 'Now look – you mustn't motor race . . . you mustn't climb that mountain . . . you mustn't go swimming.' Who is going to do that? Who has got the right to say that you can't? There's enough interference in personal freedom as it is. We keep having more and more rules and that's one of them I wouldn't like to see. The moment that comes, half the aim and incentive will have gone out of life.

I had a fabulous finish with Jimmy Clark during the *Daily Express* May meeting at Silverstone. I'd had a lot of trouble with the stub exhausts on the BRM, four of them had dropped off and they were affecting the performance of the car. The engine was lacking in puff and I was losing power and pipes all round the track.

When it started to rain towards the end of the race I began catching Jimmy who was probably easing off a bit because he knew he was in the lead with the race in his pocket. On the last lap I was only three seconds behind him and I eventually caught him as we approached the final fast corner at Woodcote. When he saw me come flying along to take him on the inside he moved over to make sure I couldn't. He was on the dry line of the track, and so I moved round on the outside of him. It was a ridiculous thing to do because I was going at a hell of a lick and this took me off the dry line on to the wet part of the track – and into a broadside which sent me over the finishing line *sideways* – to beat him by a gnat's whisker. It was one of the most exciting finishes I've ever had and the crowd went mad.

I was delighted to have beaten Jimmy and Lotus at the

same time, but I was sorry for him. To lose when he'd virtually got the race sewn up . . . bloody hell!

My duel with Jimmy was to last the whole of the 1962 season. I won my first World Championship event after four years of Grand Prix attempts – and that was the Dutch Grand Prix. Then I went on to win the German and Italian Grands Prix.

As Bette had never been to America she came with me to the Grand Prix at Watkins Glen. If I won this it meant that I would clinch the World Championship. But Jimmy Clark beat me and that left the title wide open between him and me, with everything depending on the final race to be held in South Africa.

As things turned out I won this last race and emerged as World Champion and this made me the first British driver ever to win the World Championship in an all-English car . . . the BRM! The Championship Cup itself wasn't all that imposing to look at – but it meant so much, it didn't have to be.

4
Faster than Ever Before

When I first started racing I didn't set out to be World Champion. Having driven a racing car for the first time the limit of my ambition was to get back into one as soon as possible. Having driven in a few races I wanted to get into a works car. After that my next target was to drive in a Grand Prix. So it was a gradual process. When I won my first Grand Prix in 1962, I thought – crikey, I wouldn't mind being World Champion.

It takes some time to realize that you are, in fact, World Champion. 'World' is such a big word, but when it does sink in you begin to realize what a terrific responsibility you owe to your sport, the people who put you there, and to everybody around you. You try to conduct yourself in a manner befitting a World Champion – and that isn't easy – but it isn't until you start getting invited to events and being announced as the World Champion that you fully realize what it means.

I have a younger brother who has been in Canada for many years and has a Canadian wife. Their children were born there as well. Just after I had won the World Championship, Brian went into a big car showroom in Vancouver and saw an enormous picture of me in the BRM, on the wall. When he pointed out that it was his brother the salesman said: 'Yeah? – and I'm the Prime Minister.'

Brian got quite a good thing going in the end and wrote: 'I've got fifty quid on in bets with people who won't believe you're my brother. Come over and prove it.'

Doing or becoming anything for the first time gives an immense amount of pleasure – and you also benefit financially from being World Champion. I'm not going to tell you how much money I made out of it – but a lot of things start to build up. The advertising helps to push products, as well as your own name, and more people become interested in you – and the organizers of the circuits pay more starting money for the World Champion to appear at their races.

You're asked to make public appearances all over the place and you have to make a lot of speeches. I enjoy making speeches – but they ruin my dinner. I gear myself up for a speech in much the same way that I do before a motor race. I never write a speech before the occasion – I think about it during the dinner. It helps me get the atmosphere of the occasion and the people.

Bette always feels sorry for anyone sitting either side of me when I've got to make a speech, because I cut myself off while I'm working out what to say, and I'm the most awful company. I just sit there with no sociability or chat, and scribble notes on the menu.

I acquired this method of preparing speeches at the occasion, rather than before it, quite by accident. It was at a Lotus dinner dance when I first started to drive for them. I hadn't prepared my speech because I didn't know how to. So I had to do something about it at the dinner. I was so nervous I couldn't eat. Rather than risk making a balls of it by talking off the cuff, I started scribbling a few notes on the menu.

Bette was sitting next to me and knew I was suffering agonies. To help, she kept trying to bring me into the conversation with the people sitting near by, but I didn't want to know. I was far too occupied thinking and making notes.

When I got up to make my speech an old mate, Cliff Davis, threw a bread roll at me. It missed but knocked over my glass of wine and spilt the contents all over the menu. It smudged the notes so badly I couldn't read a word. I was forced to talk off the top of my head and, to my amazement, brought the house down. I had the audience in the palm of my hands – and I knew then that if I'd prepared my speech in detail beforehand I would probably have fallen flat on my face with it.

In my study at home I've got a plaque which says: 'Graham Hill – World's First Supersonic Grand Prix Champion – 10th July 1963'. It was given to me by the 78th Tactical Fighter Squadron of the American Air Force when they were based at Woodbridge, Suffolk. After I became World Champion they asked me if I would go along to one of their dinners and give them a speech, and promised they would take me through the sound barrier if I agreed.

The first flight I had ever had up to then – other than flying sedately in airliners to and from motor races all over the world – was in a light aircraft belonging to a friend who flew me over New Zealand. So this was an offer I couldn't resist. When I arrived at the base they gave me a coffee and someone walked in with a flying helmet done up in my London Rowing Club colours, also my racing colours. I thought that was very splendid of them. Then they took me up in a Sabre jet.

When the pilot opened the throttles we took off like a whippet. The moment we were airborne he stood it on its tail and . . . whoosh . . . we shot straight up to 40 000 feet. When he levelled out we seemed to be sitting still on top of the world without any impression of speed or movement. It was marvellous . . . until he started going through a whole series of manoeuvres. Then I felt quite sick. I could feel the coffee coming up again.

'Howdya feel?' the pilot shouted.

I looked at my cockpit. It was so clean I daren't disgrace myself – so I switched on the intercom and told him I wasn't terribly well.

'Okay, I'll steady out for a bit – but don't touch that handle back there otherwise you'll eject and go sailing into orbit.'

Before I had time to be frightened he came back over the intercom.

'Right – now we go through the sound barrier.'

As we went into a dive I clutched the seat with my eyes glued on the dials whizzing round on the panel. We seemed to zoom forever.

'When are we going through the sound barrier?' I asked.

He said we had already been through it – and then my cockpit started to fill with smoke.

'We seem to be on fire,' I told him as we continued to dive.

'That's condensation – I'll soon get rid of that.'

A blast of hot air hit the back of my neck and, in seconds, all the small clouds that had formed in the cockpit disappeared. As we pulled out of the dive I noticed that we were over the Snetterton motor race track in Norfolk.

'We'll just do a quick lap,' he said, and as he stood the jet on its wing we whistled round the circuit in seconds. It was great.

I experienced tremendous G, or gravity, forces during that flight – but we're also subject to all sorts of centrifugal forces – cornering, braking and acceleration forces – when we're motor racing. If you sit in a chair for two hours or so bracing yourself like a piece of spring steel against these forces you'll feel pretty tired at the end of it. That's what we have to do in motor racing, to brace ourselves against all these G forces. We also have to control the steering wheel and work the pedals and make the gear changes, so we expend a lot of energy. The physical and mental strain in Grand Prix driving is enormous. It varies from circuit to circuit, and it pays to be fit. I've always done exercises at home, including weight-lifting, as well as breathing exercises. You can get very breathless in a racing car if you don't keep your breathing in good trim. I took up several recreational sports later in my career but around this time I played a fair bit of squash and table-tennis which are both fast games. I was racing every week-end, practising for two days and racing the third, and that kept me pretty active.

Total concentration is also needed in racing driving (and in ordinary driving for that matter). When you're hurtling along at 180 m.p.h. you need 100 per cent concentration. If you lose concentration you'll make mistakes and you'll also go slower. It's not easy to concentrate on something for any length of time. Try thinking about one thing for thirty seconds and you'll find it's difficult. So it's a technique we have to develop.

To get the best performance out of a racing car is a balancing act between centrifugal force on the corners and the driver's ability with the steering wheel and accelerator through the small patches of rubber in contact with the road through the wheels. This balancing act requires maximum concentration and in Grand Prix racing we have to keep up this concentration for two hours or more. Every time we go round a corner the centrifugal force is trying to throw the car off the corner at a tangent, like a stone on the end of a piece of string. If the string breaks the stone will fly off. So there's a helluva lot to do and think about: controlling the car and combating the elements, changing gear and getting round corners in the shortest possible time. Then there's the race itself, the messages you get from the pits and your race strategy to think about. You have to absorb the information from the pit, feed it into your brain-box mechanism and get it working to come out with the right answer.

On some circuits it's difficult to see the pit board and when you do you're usually travelling at a fair old lick and getting ready to brake for a corner coming up. If you concentrate too hard on the pit signal you could miss your braking point, fluff a gear change, or foul up the entry into the corner. So I usually just register the information and keep my concentration on my driving and the corner – and I don't start thinking about the information until I'm round the corner. In other words, I more or less photograph the message in my mind as I fly past the pits, store it there until I've gone through the corner and then start sifting the information and acting upon it.

In Grands Prix you have to drive ten-tenths most of

the time. Nine-tenths isn't good enough to win. If you're in a comfortable lead you're in a position to dictate the race at your pace. I reckon half a minute is a good distance to be in front. If you're in second or third place you must drive ten-tenths and that means you've got to concentrate like mad all the time. Quite apart from the physical side the mental effort required in concentrating is extremely tiring. If you're not physically fit – then your mental capacity is going to fall off. That's why we have to keep fit physically, as well as mentally, for racing.

I had an interesting experience some years later which centred around this business of concentration. I went to a Ford Sports Day at Brands Hatch where I drove a Capri, along with a lot of Grand Prix and other drivers. We all drew lots for the starting grid, then we jumped in the cars and belted round. They'd fitted me up with a microphone to give a commentary over the loudspeakers to the crowd while I was racing. I listened through headphones to the commentary from the stand so I knew when to come in. I was busy overtaking and trying to get among the leaders and just going through Paddock when a great booming voice said: 'COME IN GRAHAM HILL.'

There was a deathly bloody hush. I was concentrating on driving hard and it's impossible to do the two – to drive really hard and talk. I had to turn on a switch whenever I wanted to talk and I spent most of the race trying to find it. While I was talking and explaining what I was doing I found myself dropping back in the field. I just wasn't driving ten-tenths. I could drive nine-tenths but that wasn't enough. It just shows the sort of concentration required when driving a car.

I seldom talk when I'm driving on the road. If somebody wants to talk it annoys me and I automatically start driving a lot slower than I would be if I were on my own. If I'm going to a circuit with Bette, which might be a three- or four-hour drive, I might not say more than about a dozen words during the whole course of that journey. I enjoy driving a car on the road, even round London – but it's still important to concentrate.

I'm sure everyone, and I include myself, has driven a journey and arrived at the other end without remembering the places passed through. This is because we were not concentrating. We were probably driving at a steady pace without much attention. At times like these our reactions are slower, our anticipation suffers and that can be dangerous. Anticipation is tied in very closely with concentration. A goal-keeper needs good anticipation and so does a wicket-keeper, and the same thing applies in motoring.

You can sit beside a driver and tell he hasn't got any anticipation. A situation is creating itself ahead of him and by now he should be taking some sort of action. But no – he goes steaming on – and then has to stand on the brakes or take sudden avoiding action which would have been quite unnecessary if he had been concentrating on the situation developing. All this is linked with experience, of course. The more experienced one is, the easier it is to recognize a situation developing.

When we're driving Formula 1 we know all the chaps around us are experts in their field. As we're driving with experts we know what to expect of them. But in some races there are local drivers who haven't world class experience. We've never driven against them before and so we don't know what to expect from them. We give those drivers a lot of room and we're extra careful about overtaking them or racing with them. This is the same sort of technique that you have to apply on the road. You don't know who is around you. You don't know the ability of the drivers in the other cars, or the car's performance, or the condition of the tyres. So to keep safe, you have to make allowances.

I'm often asked if I mind being driven by other people. If I think the person I'm with is driving over his head, beyond his ability, I sense it. You can always tell when someone is driving too fast – the horns come up. They start making little errors – so I ask them to slow down. If they don't slow down I take the key out. At least that's what I used to do – but don't try it now because on most cars the steering locks and then you're in trouble. If it comes to the point when you've had enough – tell the driver you're getting out. Normally, when I get in a car it makes the driver nervous. Once they are nervous they make mistakes and get even more nervous. I try not to notice it. I whistle a tune, try looking out of the window, read the paper or something. But if they continue to drive badly I speak pretty sharply. That's usually enough. I don't do it all that often and I reckon I'm a reasonable passenger if the driver's all right.

Whenever Jimmy Clark drove me I'd sit quiet, trusting him completely. If he made a mistake I said nothing. He didn't appreciate this because when he made a mistake he'd shout across and say, 'For Pete's sake, why don't you *say* something?' We shared the driving once from Cologne to Monte Carlo and back in a saloon car for a special promotion and when it came to my turn at the wheel he hated being driven. It was all right when he went to sleep but when he was awake he was always on the edge of his seat, biting his nails, and shouting for me to watch out.

Like many husbands I'm not keen on being driven by my wife. It's not because Bette isn't a good driver – she's excellent, and I mean that. She's got her own car and she has, in fact, only driven me about half a dozen times down to the shops or something since we were married. I think she gets a little nervous when I'm sitting beside her in the passenger's seat. Normally, when I'm going anywhere there doesn't seem to be that much time so I drive myself.

I was asked during a talk at a university, once, whether complete strangers cowered in the passenger's seat when I stopped to give them a lift?

'It depends on what I was trying to do to them,' I told them.

I suppose I drive fairly fast, faster than average, but I try to do it smoothly so my passage is unnoticed. If anybody recognizes me it's bit embarrassing if I've made a pig's ear of it. The trouble is, when they do recognize me, they try to race me – and driving on the roads isn't supposed to be competitive. Racing drivers get rid of their competitive spirit on the track and when we come out on the roads we're generally quiet, law-abiding citizens.

As it happens, I feel I'm a lot nearer to an accident when I'm driving at 50 m.p.h. on a Sunday afternoon in the summer in England than I would if there was no speed limit. I fully appreciate the need for a 30 m.p.h. limit in some built-up areas, but in most cases I'm opposed to the 50 m.p.h. or 70 m.p.h. limits or whatever they are – on the grounds of safety. Some time after I won the Championship I'd been abroad for a few months racing – and when I came back I found there were great convoys of traffic going along the main roads nose to tail. I scooted past that lot and then found a long stretch of road with no cars on it at all and I had some very nice motoring. Before long, though, I came to another convoy. Then I saw the 50 m.p.h. signs cropping up and I realized what was happening. The limits had been introduced while I'd been away – so I slowed down and kept within the law like everyone else.

In my opinion, all this sort of limit does is bottle everyone up at the same speed. When travelling nose to tail, concentration goes – and there's just that much more chance of an accident.

5

Build-up before a Race

The reactions at the start of the Le Mans twenty-four-hour race have always puzzled me. You don't start the race sitting in the cockpit. You line up and stand in individual painted circles on the opposite side of the track to your car. There's a tremendous race atmosphere, with up to 400000 present, and a sea of faces everywhere and it's all very colourful and exciting. As the starter's flag goes up about five seconds before the 'Off' most of the drivers adopt a runner's attitude with their legs stretched like catapults. When the flag drops there's a terrific stampede of feet across the road to the cars. I can never understand why everybody runs. It's a twenty-four-hour race and if they walked it wouldn't make much difference to the eventual outcome of the race. Everybody seems wound up, and the very fact that they've run to their cars means their hearts are pounding and this is where the flap sets in. They make mistakes getting into their cars. They don't open the door properly. One driver short-cut this once by vaulting over the door and putting his leg straight through the steering wheel. He got so tangled that he ended with the gear-lever up his trouser leg.

To start any race het-up is fatal and this is where the mistakes in driving creep in. So even in Grands Prix, where we all take off *in* our cars from grid positions, I like to keep cool and not hurry. If I get into the car quietly I'll stay calm and alert for the start and the race itself.

I think we all get the 'butterflies' before a race. I know

I did before each of the 176 Grands Prix I competed in. I'm not a nervous sort of person. It's not nerves, it's apprehension really. You're about to do a performance and you want to do a great job. Everyone who performs in front of other people knows this feeling – whether they're an actor on the stage, the conductor of an orchestra, or about to make a speech, or whatever. They've been called upon to do something to prove themselves in front of other people in some way or another and they're going to have to put on a performance which is going to take a lot of effort on their part. They become apprehensive because they're aware that they mustn't let themselves or anyone else down.

Athletes feel this apprehension, of course, so it's natural for racing drivers to feel it before a race too. You try to disguise it, but it shows in different ways. Some people talk a lot and wave their arms about; others make jokes. I, personally, go very quiet and don't particularly want to talk to anybody. The only other sport I had any real success with was rowing – and I used to get the 'butterflies' far more in rowing than motor racing. I'd go pretty quiet and the 'butterflies' or 'needle', as we called it, would affect me from about three days before the event.

The blokes I rowed with used to say I was *impossible*. I didn't want to talk and I didn't want to eat, but only to be on my own so that I could build myself up to the event – as I did, later, in motor racing. Anyone who saw me at the circuits before races said I went into an almost total withdrawal and that I'd cut anyone who spoke to me. I'm not unsociable but I just didn't want to make any unnecessary effort. I wanted to save everything for the race.

The build-up used to start when I woke up on the morning of the race and wherever I was, at home or in a hotel, I'd switch off from everything other than the job in hand and start with a quiet, gentle breakfast. If Bette was with me she never spoke to me. She understood the importance of this building-up process. Once I got to the track the only people I wanted around were my team manager and the mechanics.

I know I've caused embarrassment when people came up to me in the pits and wanted to talk. I'm told I'd just look straight through them. I didn't intend to be rude – they'd just chosen the wrong moment. I'm sure people used to say things to me that I never heard, which probably was just as well as no doubt they were uncomplimentary.

It's a bit difficult to avoid interviewers when they thrust microphones right under your nose, though. One commentator came up just before a race and asked:

'Do you ever wake up in the morning, Graham, and feel like jacking it all in?'

'No, why . . . do you?' I said, and he faded away.

Athletes about to compete in an important national or international event don't want to be interrupted or engaged in small talk when they're getting ready and warming up beside the track – and that's how I feel about motor racing. Bette understood this and she wouldn't come near me until an hour before the race. Then she'd just pop into the pits, give me a peck and say: 'Good luck, darling – keep safe.'

After she'd left, if I was happy with the preparation of the car and everything, I'd often sit in the pits on a pile of tyres or something with my knees under my chin. I can doze anywhere. People laughed at this, apparently, because they knew I'd always be the last one on the grid. My car would be up there with the rest of the team waiting for me – and this baffled many people. If I was so meticulous about building myself up for the event, how come I wasn't first on the grid? My answer is that if I had made a point of being first I would have to be a highly-strung person – and I'm not.

I wasn't able to offer much of a challenge in defending my title in 1963. Jimmy Clark and Lotus won the Championship very convincingly, and I was runner-up. One extra Grand Prix was added to the series, the Mexican, and Jimmy won that. In fact, he won seven of the ten Grands Prix; Surtees won the German one – and I won Monaco and the American one. But apart from that, and coming first in the Tourist Trophy race at Goodwood, I didn't have any other wins.

The next few years were to bring about several hat-tricks, though, while I was still driving for BRM. I won the Monaco Grand Prix three times on the trot as well as the American Grand Prix. That was through 1963, 1964 and 1965, and I was runner-up in the World Championship Title during those same three years. I also won the Tourist Trophy for the second time, and the Rheims twelve-hour race for the first time.

People often ask me which were my most satisfying races. This is always a tricky one to answer. I think there were about five during my career but I don't want to pull out all the goodies now as three of them came later. In the period covered so far I would say that the highlights were the hat-trick at Monaco in 1965 and the German Grand Prix in 1962.

I didn't mention the German race at the Nürburgring when describing my Championship year as I wanted to save it until now. It was run in torrential rain with zero visibility from start to finish. When the flag dropped my BRM went like a dream and I managed to get into the lead early on – hotly pursued by Dan Gurney's Porsche and John Surtees's Lola. We were never more than five seconds apart during the whole of the two and three quarter hours. But with that sort of pressure from Dan and John, on a circuit about fourteen miles long with rises and falls of something like 1 000 feet, surrounded by woods and trees and with 187 corners, I was well aware that I could easily make a mistake in the wet. I had to concentrate like mad and by the time the race was over, and I had won, I was completely drained both mentally and physically. It was one of the best races I'd driven up to that point and it had me set fair for my first World Championship that year.

The car that took me to my third Monaco victory in 1965 was one of the nicest looking BRMs ever built. The road circuit through the streets and round the houses at Monte Carlo is one of the trickiest in the world. When you're racing on relatively narrow tracks with sharp corners it's not easy to overtake. You need to get into the lead as soon as possible and then keep there. My BRM had put up the fastest time in practice so I started from the pole position and got off to a flier without any problems and continued to lead for the first twenty-four laps. Then I came across a back-marker as I came over the brow of the hill towards the chicane. I was doing about 120 m.p.h. with this other car limping slowly towards the chicane, with some sort of mechanical trouble, and it was obvious he would be blocking the chicane at the precise moment I wanted to go through it. I couldn't get there first and I couldn't slow down in time to let him through ahead of me, so I braked as hard as I could and shot up the escape road. The engine stalled as I came to a halt and I had to get out and push the car backwards on to the track.

This lost me thirty seconds or so and dropped me back into fifth place. By now Lorenzo Bandini and John Surtees had their Ferraris in what seemed to be an impregnable position. I was pretty annoyed at this but there was still three-quarters of the race to go and I chased after them and gradually reduced their lead. I broke the lap record several times as I carved through the field and at about half distance I managed to take Surtees for second place. Only Bandini was ahead and as I gradually closed the gap I had several attempts at overtaking him; but the Italian was giving no quarter. This led to a terrific duel before I finally got by him and put the BRM back into the lead with thirty-three laps to run.

The two-and-a-half-hour race ended at a new record race average of 74·34 m.p.h. It was enormously satisfying to have won a race in which I'd had to stop and get out and push. What made it even more satisfying was that both Stirling Moss and Fangio were there to see me pull off my third win in three consecutive years.

1965 was a good year. Just before the Monaco Grand Prix our youngest daughter, Samantha, was born to complete our family of Brigitte (6) and Damon (4). I love children and wherever I go in the world they are always trailing after me. Bette reckons I'm a sort of Pied Piper.

John Coombs, for whom I'd done a lot of saloon car and Formula 2 driving, agreed to be her godfather and we asked Eba Grant and Doreen Leston to be godmothers. Lots of motor racing folk came to the christening that autumn in our local church and we ended with a tremendous party in our garden afterwards.

Something else happened that year which also gave me enormous pleasure. I learned to fly in a Chipmunk at Elstree airfield and spent a lot of time there.

6

Indianapolis 500

I mentioned earlier that Bette understood my necessity to be quiet before a race and that she wished me luck and said 'Keep safe' an hour before. She never said she hoped I'd win. She's not superstitious but she never mentioned winning . . . *except once*. That was in 1966 when I went to America for the Indianapolis 500. She didn't come with me but saw the race via satellite in a cinema at Hammersmith which showed it live. Just before race day she asked the two elder children what to say in the telegram she was sending to wish me luck. Brigitte said 'We hope you win the race' – so Bette sent this telegram: 'Good luck, darling. We hope you win the race'.

The Indianapolis 500-mile race is rather complicated and goes on more or less for the whole month of May with testing and qualification trials. The two-and-a-half-mile track is oblong with four corners which are exactly the same theoretically but all different in reality. There's a windsock there to check on, and if the wind is blowing differently on a particular day it makes a big difference to the times and corners.

There's a tremendous mystique built up about the race and everybody talks about it in slightly mystical terms which prevents everyone from going fast – and you have to overcome this. It's as though there's a wall, an invisible speed barrier. They get up to 160 m.p.h. and for some reason, that's it. It happened to me and I got to 155 . . . 159 . . . 160 m.p.h. and I *couldn't* go any faster. I had to sit down and think about it, and then one day . . .

47

Pow . . . I was doing 167 m.p.h., just like that and then 170 m.p.h. It's extraordinary, just a mental thing.

They make you do a 'rookie' test in which you have to start off doing ten laps at 140 m.p.h., then ten at 150 m.p.h. but they won't let you do both on the same day in case you get exhausted. This is the way they build it up and you think it's a lot of cobblers. Then you think: 'Well, bloody hell, perhaps they're right.' I remember one meeting where all the rookies had finished and passed their tests when an old hand came in and said to one of them: 'You drifted out a bit too high up the wall out there, Bud. Got to watch the line and keep it in the group.' They give you all this stuff and you don't know what they're talking about half the time. Then another bloke came in and said: 'The one thing you've got to remember is – you'll never win Indianapolis first time.' That boosted our morale a lot!

The race is billed as the richest, fastest and most dangerous motor race in the world and attracts a quarter of a million spectators. The cars roll off the starting grid keeping formation behind a pace car for two warming-up laps and then, as they cross the starting line, they accelerate into the first turn. I had never been in this kind of start before and as we passed the start line and the green flag dropped we were all doing about 100 m.p.h. I was on the outside of the fifth row at the start and we'd only gone a few yards when two cars touched and set off a massive holocaust within the closely-packed bunch of thirty-three cars accelerating like mad into the first corner. There were cars in pieces all over the place, bits tumbling out of the sky and all hell was let loose. Eleven cars were demolished and I just managed to get through this whirling mass of destruction, with one other car on my tail. We were the last two cars to get clear. The race, which was only three seconds old, became known as 'the year of the big shunt'. Incredibly, no one was hurt.

The race was stopped and then, after about ninety minutes spent clearing up the wreckage, we re-started. Someone spun on some oil on the track just in front of

ABOVE 1. *This Is Your Life* – a well-kept secret. Father, Mother, Bette and Eamonn Andrews

RIGHT 2. The most important race of my life – even though the bicycle was fixed to the floor.

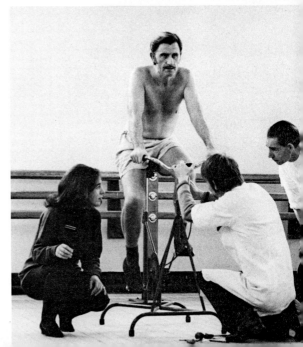

TOP OPPOSITE 3. You were pretty close to the accident in those early Formula 3 days.

BOTTOM OPPOSITE 4. With Colin Chapman in 1967, the year before I won the World Championship for the second time.

RIGHT 5. My third win at Monaco but it took a push up the escape road to do it.

BELOW 6. Any country that does well in motor racing has a wonderful shop window – and the wise ones hang their hat on it.

7. Dan Gurney, Jack Brabham, Bruce McLaren, Richie Ginther, Denny Hulme, Jochen Rindt. The stakes are high in motor racing and there just isn't room for pettiness.

8. No one was hurt in this sixteen-car pile-up which was incredible. The Indianapolis 500 in 1966.

me and I thought we were in for another shunt – but we all missed him. Anyway, I pressed on to fight my way up the field and when Jimmy Clark spun a couple of times I found myself in second place. Jackie Stewart was in the lead by a comfortable margin, with only a few laps to go, then his engine broke and I inherited the lead. That's the way it stayed and I won.

They make a tremendous fuss about the winner at Indianapolis. There's a black-and-white chequered carpet and girls and television cameras and all that jazz – and a great glass of milk that you have to drink. There had been a bit of confusion during the race, what with the big shunt early on and then the re-start, and this had upset the lap scorers and score board. During the last few laps, Jimmy Clark's pit held out boards that he was winning and my pit was telling me that I was winning. While I was on the winner's dais one of the officials came up and suggested that it was possible that I might not be the winner. I *knew* I'd beaten Jimmy – so I just looked at this questioning chap deadpan and said: 'No way, mate – I drank the milk!' Then blow me if Jimmy didn't come in half a lap later and drive into the winner's circle thinking he'd won. He forced his way through the crowd and tugged my sleeve and said, 'Who won?' I had a girl on each arm (that was all part of the trimmings) so I looked at each in turn and then at the crowd around me and said to Jimmy: 'Well, if I haven't I don't know what all these people are doing.'

Everyone agreed in the end that I had won and I was awarded the 160000 dollars purse. The incredible thing is that within minutes they presented me with a newspaper with the headline – GRAHAM HILL THE WINNER – across the front page complete with photographs. I don't know how they managed it but I was terribly impressed. They must have been setting it up during the race and maybe they printed pages with other winners too. Anyway, when the prize-giving came round they capped it by giving me the actual metal printer's plate of that front page and it's something I have treasured ever since.

Indianapolis is obviously a very satisfying race to win, particularly that one as it was the first time a rookie had won it first time out for forty years. It was good to receive that telegram from Bette and the children saying: 'We hope you win.' It was the first time she'd ever mentioned winning before a race – and it worked. It was also good to nip over there and collect all that loot from under their very noses. I used the money to buy my first private plane.

Somebody wins Indi every year – but nobody can actually put doors on the loos any more because that's one of the things I did over there. During the practice one of the top organizers bumped into me and said: 'Hello, old man, whadya think of our little circuit here?'

'Well, there are two things wrong with it,' I told him, 'You run it the wrong way round – and there are no doors on the loos. It's the one place I like to be private – and I think it's embarrassing, indecent and undignified.'

By 6.30 next morning he had the whole lot fitted with doors. I think that was quite an achievement.

I wonder if you saw the MGM film *Grand Prix*. We had a lot of fun making that in 1966. I only had a small part and if you blinked you probably missed me. When Hollywood took over I remember saying to John Frankenheimer, the film's director: 'Look, there's *no way* you can make this film. You can't close Monte Carlo for three weeks. They'll never agree to that!'

Well, he did and he really excelled himself and got some fabulous racing shots. In some other scenes, filmed at the French Grand Prix circuit at Clermont-Ferrand, the script called for me to follow James Garner round the track. He was the star playing the lead in the film and just before we set off John Frankenheimer came up to me and said: 'For God's sake don't push him – don't push him.' I looked across to James Garner some distance away and there he was with his helmet on, puffing away on a cigarette, all tweaked up. 'Think of the insurance – think of the insurance,' said Frankenheimer, 'don't push him.'

I said 'okay, okay,' and got in the car and they waved us away – and I never saw James Garner again. He really fancied himself at this motor racing business. He was very keen and not bad either. It was amazing. I only wish I was as good at his job as he was at mine.

I was very impressed with the technical innovations they introduced while we were on location. To get shots of a car spinning they had a bloody great platform mounted on wheels, with the top half of the body of a racing car on the turntable, for towing behind another car. The idea was to put one of the film stars, an Italian, I think, into this thing and tow it behind a high-powered car round the circuit at an astronomical rate. Then, at some convenient moment, they'd release a spring to send the turntable whizzing round with the mock-up racing car on it and the unfortunate driver inside. I was terrified just to look at the thing and you can imagine what would have happened if the ball races had broken. They had a hell of a job to get this actor chap into the thing. By the time they did, he looked so shit-scared that it rather buggered up the effect – he was supposed to be the big, brave hero.

I think the racing scenes in the film were terrific. The story was a bit weak but that was partly due to looking at it through motor racing's eyes. The film makers know what's box office, what brings people in, so you've got to allow them the licence. After all it's their money and as long as our bit is good I don't think we've any reason for complaints. Most of it was fabulous.

The Belgian Grand Prix at Spa had a bit of drama to it later that season. When it came on to rain cars began to spin. I managed to get past them but shortly afterwards I spun round like a top myself. When I came to a stop at the side of the road I saw Jackie Stewart's BRM in the ditch. He looked in a bad way so I ran over to see if I could help. He was in considerable pain trapped by the side of the car which had been pushed in. The petrol tanks had ruptured and he was covered with petrol. There was a big risk of fire and I turned off the fuel pump switches and then tried to lift him out. Petrol burns the skin badly and one way and another he was pretty dazed. The steering wheel was jammed up against his leg and it was obvious that this would have to be removed before I could get him out.

It took twenty-five minutes to release Jackie and get him off to hospital in an ambulance. That's one nightmare everyone can do without – being trapped in a car with fuel spilling all over the place, knowing that at any moment just one tiny spark could set the whole thing off.

I left BRM at the end of the year to rejoin Colin Chapman and Lotus. I'd been with BRM for seven years and I thought I'd better move in case they painted me over. People can get so used to you that they go deaf if you keep complaining about something. It was a difficult choice to make, but we parted on the best of terms. I was very happy to become joint number one driver with Jimmy Clark at Lotus.

7
World Champion – Second Time

There were a lot of break-downs during 1967, my first year with Lotus; but things improved dramatically in 1968. The season started on New Year's Day at the South African Grand Prix with my team-mate Jimmy Clark coming in first, and me second. I went on to win the Spanish Grand Prix and then the Monaco Grand Prix which made it my fourth win there.

It's always exciting for those who follow motor racing to have a closely fought Championship lasting through the season, and better still if the climax comes in the final Grand Prix. It's tense for the drivers – and this is precisely what happened in 1968 with a story-book finish to the season at Mexico. I had thirty-nine Championship points, Jackie Stewart thirty-six and Denny Hulme thirty-three. If Jackie won the race he would win the Championship. As the two days of practice wore on I began to get more and more intense and withdrawn and became pretty anti-social. That's one of the reasons why Bette didn't come over. I knew I was going to be pretty mean and there was just the chance I might have taken it out on her. I don't like that kind of unpleasantness and prefer to be alone under such conditions.

The circuit in Mexico is 7300 feet up and this takes a bit of getting used to but the altitude problem is the same for all the cars and drivers. The race turned into a ding-dong battle and by lap five Jackie Stewart was in the lead, with me behind him and Denny Hulme in third place. Then Denny had an accident coming off the banking on lap eleven when a rear shock absorber broke and he lost control. Meanwhile, I had got past Jackie Stewart and increased my lead in the later stages as he started to fall back with a misfiring engine. I went on to win and, thus, followed up my previous success in 1962 – by becoming World Champion for the second time.

Lotus-Ford did well, taking first, third and sixth places in that race; but the year was marred by the most appalling tragedy when Jimmy Clark was killed at Hockenheim. No one could foresee Jimmy having an accident such as this, in a Formula 2 race of all things, for he was the complete maestro who stood among the immortals in the sport alongside drivers like Fangio and Stirling Moss.

I was only a few seconds behind Jimmy but I didn't see it happen. It had been raining and when I arrived on the scene all I saw were some tyre marks leading off the track into the trees. I couldn't see how or why they had gone off and assumed that two cars must have touched, because at that particular point in the circuit there was no reason for any car to go off.

When I finished the race and they told me that it was Jimmy – it took some while to sink in. It's obviously a great shock when a team-mate, who is also a close friend gets killed. It leaves a void and you wonder how you can keep going – but, of course, you do. When I flew back to Elstree I remember Keith Smith coming over to me while I was still sitting in my aircraft. We'd often flown to race meetings at home and abroad together. He'd just been on a local flight and when he came over to greet me he said: 'What about poor old Jim?' I continued filling in my log-book, without looking up, and said: 'Yeah . . . it was terrible.' That probably seems abrupt; it wasn't meant to be, but it was all the emotion I could afford to show. I was terribly upset over Jimmy's death but, as a racing driver, I couldn't allow my emotions to come through. If I did I would have been lost and unable to cope – and I'm sure all racing drivers feel the same. You may feel the loss deeply and grieve inwardly – but it must never be allowed to get on top of you. Time is the big healer, of course, and there's another thing . . . when a racing driver gets killed, you remind yourself that they died doing what they most enjoyed.

Just what caused Jimmy's accident we'll never know. It certainly wasn't driver error. Nobody has satisfactorily explained why Stirling Moss went straight off the track at Goodwood and no one is ever likely to come up with the answer to this one. There was one eye-witness, a marshal, standing just about at that point of the track. He wrote in his report that he had seen the car coming towards him normally, then it started to snake. The back slid out to one side, then the other and the car veered off the track sideways into the trees killing Jimmy instantly.

Jimmy thoroughly enjoyed and made the best of his life. He was brought up on a farm and this was a complete contrast to his life as a racing driver. He always enjoyed going back to his home in Scotland and the simpler ways of life. His skill at motor racing took him into the limelight and it was very touching to find somebody who wasn't hard and cynical, who basically was a warm, honest person. Being shy, he hated making speeches, and he had to work hard at it to build his confidence. Although shy in the presence of other people, he was always confident in the element of racing, but not over-confident – and very competitive.

The combination of Colin Chapman and Jimmy Clark had been an extremely successful one. You've got to tie the two together because Colin designed the cars and Jimmy raced them. It was a parallel success story, with each complementing the other.

After Jimmy's death, the Lotus team was in despair and Colin Chapman seriously considered giving up racing. He had always said he would stop the day Jimmy Clark stopped racing. Jimmy had been killed in April. The next Grand Prix was the Spanish, in May. It made me more determined than ever to go out and win that one. I think that victory made Colin and Lotus think it was worth carrying on. Colin said he would continue until the end of the year and see how he felt about things then. I'm glad he did, otherwise I wouldn't have won the Championship and Colin wouldn't still be racing now.

If you're a racing driver and married – one thing's sure. You can't do it unless your wife is 100 per cent behind you. I could never have won those two World Championships if Bette had just been tolerating my driving. She was *with* me all the way and never once suggested I should stop. You don't have to be married to be a racing driver, of course, but most of us are and I'm all for it. Marriage has a maturing effect. The wives have a tough time because they must feel apprehensive about the dangers; that's only natural. In a way it's worse for them than us. But Bette never bothered me with any of her anxieties. She liked me to win and I think she was more disappointed than I was if I didn't.

Bette has a very strong personality and she used to stand up to me over many things early on. When you get two people with strong wills in a marriage it often leads to fireworks. She had a strong Victorian upbringing and her parents were very close but firm, and her father was Boss. He had four daughters and he could so easily have succumbed to them and his wife. This is how Bette came to see my position in our home. If two people try to be boss in the home it usually destroys them – and the children. Bette went along with me and my ideas and accepted me as the breadwinner and assisted me in my racing career in every way possible and I'm grateful to her for that.

She gave me the freedom to go out and race. She had to take the boot on many occasions – and often in front of people – but that's marriage. I'd sometimes use her as a buffer, even when it wasn't her fault, and, of course, it hurt her. Whenever I realized this I'd apologize and try to make up for it later. She would never have walked out on me and the children in difficult times. She just didn't believe in that and it was comforting for me to know this, and also that I had her blessing all the way in my racing. She always said I worked at everything but our marriage. I'd be the first to agree with that. I fully appreciate a woman *does* have to work at a marriage, and that she puts in 90 per cent of effort to make it a success – with the man adding his 10 per cent . . . if he's willing.

Bette loves motor racing, the atmosphere and the people, and came to my races whenever she could. She did my time-keeping during the practices. She's very good at it and was able to time at least twelve to fourteen different cars, with one stopwatch, when they were all going round at the same time. This was a great help because when I came into the pits I could see how my competitors' times were coming down and what sort of progress they were making. She did the timing during the races as well. It kept her absorbed and it was far better for her to be occupied than sit there and let anxieties creep in.

I'm not the type to bring home chocs, in fact the only time I ever took flowers home they were just daisies I'd picked hurriedly in the garden. Nevertheless, I reckon I'm a family man. Bette and the children have always been my sheet-anchors. My happiest moments are at home with her, and romping around the garden with the children. Because I enjoy motor racing I haven't been able to have as much home life, or private life, as I would have liked. When you become World Champion, tremendous demands are made on your time. When I won the final race in Mexico which gave me the 1968 Championship title I arrived home at 11 a.m. and was off again by mid-day to make a speech at a lunch in London. That gave me just one hour with Bette. At the height of the racing season there's a Grand Prix, or some race, most week-ends. Two days or so are usually taken up with practice and then there's the travelling time which, if the race is in South Africa or Australia, takes up another day or two.

One is expected to do all sorts of television and radio interviews and shows, films for the motoring and oil companies, besides attending a mass of functions and making speeches all over the place, including abroad. All these claims on one's time cut right through one's private life. Bette often asked me when I would be home so she could give a dinner party or something – and when I looked at my diary I'd give her a date in three months' time. She'd say that was ridiculous – and have to arrange it without me. I think she would be quite surprised at the number of public engagements I did refuse so that I could have an occasional day or evening at home with her and the family. Although she was put out, she didn't press the point. Like me, she felt that motor racing had given us everything as well as a great amount of pleasure – so it was only right that we should give back something.

One of the things I really enjoyed was to hop in my aeroplane and fly off to give a chat to a troop of Boy Scouts, when asked. I was one myself and always liked it when sportsmen came to our troop in Hendon to give us a talk. We raved about it for months afterwards. My years spent as a Boy Scout were some of the most enjoyable of my life. As with motor racing, I felt I owed the Scouts something and, this way, I could give a little of that something back. Incidentally, I used to play the drums in the Scout band, but I've never been asked to repeat the performance.

I always try to arrange my appointments to give some time to the Springfield Boys' Club at Upper Clapton in London. This is motor racing's boys' club and it has always had fantastic support from firms and individuals connected with the sport, and from other friends of the Club. There wasn't much a boy could do with his spare time in that part of London's East End and that's why the Club was formed. Every night and every week-end, the Club help a hundred or so of the local lads get more out of life by putting more in. The Club has carpentry shops where they can build their own canoes, or make furniture, a garage workshop for them to maintain the Club's go-karts, a billiards room, table-tennis, a gym, trampoline, badminton court, and canteen. All these, as well as summer camps and expeditions, fishing, archery, driving lessons, and community aid projects. You name it, the Club provides it.

Jimmy Clark, John Surtees, Jack Brabham, Denny Hulme, Bruce McLaren, Charles Lucas, Les Leston, Mike Hailwood, Peter Gethin, Jo Sieff, Piers Courage, Jackie Stewart and many others were all honorary members and all helped to raise a lot of money for the Club. In my first Championship year I was asked to draw the Club's weekly raffle and present the prizes. I had some excellent games of table-tennis with the boys afterwards and I thoroughly enjoyed it. Some were very promising players. That's how my link with the Club started and I've been honoured to be their President since. There's so much discord and violence these days that it's good for boys to be able to take part in such activities, and to compete in various sports and mix with people of their own, and different, ages and backgrounds.

So far as my own children were concerned I considered it equally vital to allow their characters to expand – within the confines of a certain amount of discipline, of course. No organization can run without some discipline and if children don't get it they lose respect for the people who are supposed to be giving it. If you had come to my house when the children were young you'd probably have thought there wasn't any discipline. In my view, you've got to give children plenty of rope – so long as you let them know exactly where the end of the rope is. If I was away with racing and engagements so often, one might wonder how I managed to act as father to my three children. I had certain standards. Bette had hers too and, obviously, our ideas weren't far apart and while I was away she upheld these – otherwise the whole place would have gone mad.

I can't think of anything more rewarding than bringing up a child and producing a person with whom you'd like to spend time; someone who is good company and a lot of fun. It has always given me tremendous pleasure to be able to take my children somewhere and know that they're not going to embarrass me or cause disturbance to other people. I've always tried not to swamp them. I'm very proud of my children and always enjoy their company. When they were young I loved playing with them and found it very relaxing. You can't put on an act with children – they see through it right away. You have to be natural and, in my book, there's nothing more relaxing than being natural.

One of the biggest thrills of my life was when Bette, Brigitte and Damon came with me to Buckingham Palace to receive the Order of the British Empire, awarded after I won the World Championship for the second time. I was disappointed Samantha couldn't come but she was still a bit young. The four of us went in together and it's the most magnificent place one can imagine. The paintings and tapestries and furnishings are so inspiring you can't really take it all in. The investiture itself was staged in the ballroom and it was quite something for Brigitte and Damon to *see* the sword placed by Her Royal Highness Queen Elizabeth the Queen Mother on the shoulders of those receiving their knighthoods – just like they had read in their history books. Relatives watch from the balcony and they are positioned so the children among them can get a good view. When I was called forward to receive my OBE from the Queen Mother she chatted about motor racing and it was a very moving moment.

Racing has changed a lot since I started. The cars are faster and more streamlined with more powerful engines and better fuel and oil. Tyres are wider and the negative lift from the aerofoils, which are rather like an inverted aeroplane wing providing downward pressure on the tyres to give them more grip on the track, have put the cornering speeds up. The brakes are better, too, allowing drivers to go deeper at the end of the straights before they have to brake. Drivers have to concentrate harder and the driving is a much finer balancing act than it was. You could be rougher with the older types of cars and get away with it. Nowadays the driving has to be more accurate and precise. The higher speeds also demand greater mental and physical stamina, so it's tougher on the driver. The competition is more intense and the rewards are greater.

The circuits have changed quite a bit, too, and I'm often asked which is my favourite circuit. If I had a favourite circuit it would mean that I would also have an unfavourite one and that would start me off with a psychological disadvantage. On that circuit I'd be saying to myself, 'I don't like this one so much,' and that's no way to go into a motor race. So I don't have any favourite circuits. There are some races I prefer to win, because they're more exacting and more of a driver's circuit and present a challenge through being difficult, but I don't really care where I race so long as the track is in good condition. Each circuit is different − otherwise it would be boring. They all present different problems and I get more satisfaction from doing well on the difficult circuits.

I think the Targa Florio in Sicily is the toughest course. The race is run through villages and very mountainous country with sheer drops immediately beside the road. It's narrow and slippery with loose stones flying around and takes in about 1100 corners. The circuit is difficult to remember and takes two or three years of practising and racing on to get to know. As you go round you try to recall the landmarks for each corner, a clump of trees perhaps, or a house. To make a mistake and go flying round what you believe is a fast corner, only to find it's a slow one, could be suicidal.

While the cars are practising you frequently meet people, donkeys and dogs in your path. When there are herds of cattle you come across their visiting cards on the road and the car suddenly becomes a muck-spreader. Things get more difficult when the race is on. You're concentrating on the car in front, thinking about your overtaking point and trying to remember what lies ahead at the next corner. It's one of the oldest motor races in the world. I've never won it but I've always enjoyed taking part as it provides a complete contrast to driving in Grands Prix and other races.

A great deal of the success in winning conventional races comes through setting up the car correctly, and this has to be done to suit each particular circuit. A car at Monza, which is a very fast circuit, doesn't have the same sort of set up as it does for Brands Hatch which is a very twisty, swooping, type of circuit.

When all the technical and mechanical changes have been made the driver has to put in some considerable time testing the car for behaviour in the corners on that particular circuit. He can help the designer enormously if he can tell him precisely what is wrong with the car. For instance, if a driver comes in and drops a little gem like: 'It's handling like a pig,' – the poor designer has to conjure up a picture of a pig, and then what he would do to the pig to make it corner. If a driver says, 'I think it's understeering a bit and I think it could be brought out with the rollbars,' then the designer knows exactly what's needed to improve the handling and general performance. The more experience a driver has, the more he can help the designer.

I made notes after every race to record the set-up changes I'd made and my observations at the time, so that for each circuit the following year I had a little bit of advance knowledge from which to work. This varies, of course, because we often had different cars but it provided a good starting basis. The engines have to be tuned to suit the climatic conditions on the different circuits all over the world, which vary from sea-level to over 7000 feet.

All changes have to be worthwhile and tested against the stopwatch. Sometimes I've made an alteration on a car which has produced a slightly better practice time, but in a Grand Prix lasting two hours or more it might be more difficult to drive consistently fast with it than perhaps with an easier set-up that would provide slightly slower times. All these sort of things have to be considered if races are to be won.

I'm not superstitious and I don't have a mascot or some special thing I take racing with me. The moment you do that you're in dead trouble, because if you've forgotten to bring it you will be worrying about the awful things that might happen and you won't be able to concentrate on driving. Then things will happen because, in a way, you've willed them to. Bette did buy me a St Christopher medal once, but I didn't wear it. Then she had it engraved with my blood group and allergies and as it then had a practical use I did wear it.

Motor racing is one of the few sports in which the participants can't hear the reactions of the audience. The driver can't be spurred on to greater efforts by encouragement from the crowd. His only contact with the outside world is his pit-board. But you never feel lonely – there just bloody well isn't time.

8

Four Wheels — Two Wheels

1969 was to be a pretty eventful year for me. It started with the group of formula-car races, known as the Tasman Series, with four races in New Zealand and three in Australia. I'd raced in them before but it was the first time I had ever done the complete series. I enjoyed it thoroughly and as the series is run during their summer it was good to have a break from the winter months back home. As always when I am out there, I did a bit of water-ski-ing between races. I also took up golf while I was out there this time and got hooked on the game.

I was still driving for Lotus and when the Grand Prix season came round with the first race in South Africa I only managed second place – which was a bit of an anti-climax after having won Mexico and the World Championship at the end of the previous year.

The Monaco Grand Prix was to become another highlight though. Monaco is one of the true road circuits in Grand Prix racing. It contains everything you meet on the public roads like lamp-posts, houses, hotels, trees and kerbs. The race is run through the streets and round the harbour of Monte Carlo and these are closed to normal traffic for a few days each year so the drivers can prepare for the race. It's a very short, sharp, circuit full of bends and corners and during the race you have to change gear around 1500 times. Drivers and cars take a terrific pounding.

To win any race you must have a car that's capable of

finishing and the rest is up to you. I had a good one and my win this time gave me added satisfaction as it was my fifth Monaco victory.

There were all sorts of problems during the next six Grands Prix that season.

I had handling difficulties with the car during the Dutch and French races.

After the British Grand Prix Bette and I gave a party in a marquee in the garden of our Mill Hill home. Two hundred people turned up and the drinks certainly flowed, which is more than I can say for the Silverstone race we were supposed to be celebrating where I ran out of fuel, of all things, in the closing laps.

I had trouble with the gearbox in the German Grand Prix and finished in fourth place. Then, with only five laps to go in the Italian Grand Prix when I was in second place, a halfshaft broke.

Things looked quite good for me in the Canadian Grand Prix until I went out with engine trouble; but I made my mark in the American Grand Prix. Watkins Glen is a terrific place for spectators and drivers, a real carnival occasion, and this year the organizers had raised the first prize to $50000 making it the richest Grand Prix purse ever offered.

I struggled through 90 laps of the 108-lap race with handling problems and then, when I was lying in fifth place, I spun round on some oil. As I got out to push the car and re-start the stalled engine I noticed that the rear tyres were bald and had started to 'chunk'. This accounted for the spin. When I got back into the car I had to continue without my seat belts as I couldn't do them up myself. The mechanics always fastened them for me as the cockpit was so narrow. Before I had gone far, the car's handling became even more odd. It was obvious that I would have to change the bald tyres and as I went by the pits I signalled so that they would be ready for the tyre change the next time round.

As I went along the straight on that lap, the right-hand rear tyre collapsed and the car went out of control. It veered off the track, hit a bank, rolled over and shot me out while flying backwards upside-down in the air. Apparently, I was catapulted some distance through the air before I hit the ground and rolled twenty yards beyond the wreckage. All I remember was going backwards at speed some way off the ground. I was only aware of being in the air and going fast, and I shall never know whether it was a good or bad thing that my straps weren't fastened.

The next thing that more or less came into focus was a siren; and I remember being in the ambulance. My teammate, Jochen Rindt, went on to win and collect that lovely prize. I collected something different. When I got to the Arnott Ogden Memorial Hospital in Elmira a lot of my racing friends were around me. I was fairly well drugged but I could see my legs weren't looking too good. Apparently, when I was thrown out of the car my lower legs had caught on the dashboard and the wrench had broken my right knee at the joint, and dislocated my left, and torn all the ligaments.

When the orthopaedic surgeon explained the extent of the injuries he told me that 50 per cent of patients with similar injuries suffered loss of circulation in the legs. To prevent this, it was essential in the opinion of him and his colleagues that I received immediate therapy, followed by reconstructive surgery and exploration of the nerves and a very long period of physiotherapy and rehabilitation exercises. Things got complicated by the high fever, and low blood count, that followed which needed a five-pint blood transfusion to put right.

I was in the American hospital for about two weeks and they looked after me extremely well. Bette had flown out to be with me, which was a terrific comfort, and we were together almost constantly during that time – longer than at any other time during the whole of our marriage. There was a lot of fan mail and Bette bought a whole load of greeting cards so that we could answer and send them off. I signed them and she addressed the envelopes and licked the stamps. She also took charge of my telephone and all the letter-writing to personal friends that was necessary. I think I wore her out because she came to the hospital in the morning and when it came to around midnight and she said she must go I'd ask her to stay and watch television with me. This surprised her because normally I'm a bit of a loner. But I just liked her sitting there beside me.

Things weren't so hot when the specialists told me it was unlikely I'd ever be able to get back to professional driving again. In fact, there was some serious doubt as to whether I would be able to walk without support from a stick. I reflected on this but there was no question in my mind: this was just a temporary set back and I would return to racing. While I was being treated I had to listen to their advice, of course, and go along with their recommendations.

There were some brighter moments when the students tried to break in. The authorities had set up a bit of a security wing and the big game was for the girl students to try and reach my room. Every now and again a bevy of beauties would rush in and dance up and down and say: 'We've made it.' Then they'd get me to sign something to prove it.

When we left the hospital for home the organizer of the United States Grand Prix very kindly laid on a light aircraft from Elmira to New York to meet up with a Boeing 707 flight to London due to leave at 11.30 that night. It was bitterly cold, below freezing, and I spent a lot of time lying on the stretcher on various tarmacs. The flight into New York went well and once there we were moved into one of the waiting rooms. Then they bundled me into a section of the 707 where four seats had been removed to make room for a bed of sorts.

When the plane landed at London next morning everybody and his dog seemed to be there with all the press and television. A lot of my friends had come along and they carried my stretcher off the plane, down the steps, and into the ambulance. It was hair-raising as I was sure they were going to drop me. The Ford Motor Company were extremely helpful; they supplied the ambulance and also arranged the hospital I was to go to and the surgeons who were to operate on my legs. My friends came along in the ambulance with me, with one of them driving, and it was a bit of a jolly really.

At University College Hospital in London I was given a very nice room and looked after superbly. They operated on Sunday morning to cut both knees open and tie all the ligaments up. When I came round, after four and a half hours on the table, I was in the most terrible pain. It was indescribable. They tried me on normal pain killers but when they didn't work they put me on heavy doses of heroin for a week. It killed the pain and didn't affect me in any other way – and I was immensely grateful. I had trouble sleeping and wasn't eating much. In fact I had lost a stone in weight since the accident. When the nurses came to wash me it was like strumming a guitar as their hands went over my ribs.

Bette couldn't be with me as much as in America because she had the children to look after at home. So she wrote 'Good morning, darling' on the plaster cast of one of my feet and 'Good night, darling' on the other.

The surgeons hadn't been able to straighten my bandy left leg; it was even more bent, and the other one was bent, too. But I was grateful for all they had done for me during the operation. Not so grateful, though, when they told Bette I wouldn't be racing for another year. I told them that was no good – and they complained bitterly to her about my refusing to listen to what they had to say. But I just didn't want to know about that sort of thing. I refused to believe it. If I find I want to do something, and somebody tells me that I can't or that I'm not able to, there's an added challenge and it makes me more determined. I was aiming to get back into racing for the first Grand Prix of the coming season, and that was the South African one in Johannesburg on 7 March, five months almost to the day from the time of my shunt in America.

In the meantime I knew I had to stay in hospital so I thought I might as well enjoy it. I let it be known amongst my friends that I had heard on very good authority that champagne provided a lot of calcium for healing bones. The place became flooded in champagne with corks popping all over the place but we soon got rid of it. I had some fantastic things sent to me. A motoring magazine in America pinched a bed-sheet from the local hospital and had it inscribed with masses of funny get well messages and pictures of me and my car. I got the staff at University College Hospital to hang it up on the wall in my room. It was a real work of art and brightened the place up no end.

I also received a huge envelope, about five foot square, from Gregor Grant who was the editor of *Autosport*. His family are all very musical and artistic. His daughter, Simone, is an excellent commercial photographer; and one of his sons, Don, who is a commercial artist fixed this up complete with a ten-inch stamp with Bette's head on it, representing the Queen. When I opened the envelope there was an enormous card signed by everyone in motor racing you can think of, wishing me well. It chuffed me no end and must have taken a tremendous amount of effort and organization to arrange.

Someone else sent me some pheasants. These presented a problem because I left them hanging up in my room. After a couple of days, I could see the nurses' noses beginning to twitch and they gave me one or two old-fashioned looks. They cast their eyes around the room – but couldn't see the pheasants. Eventually, I had them hung out of the window. They could be seen from the street, apparently, because the chef sent up a message to say that if I cared to send them down he'd cook them for me. It must have looked a bit odd to see a brace of pheasants hanging outside the window of a hospital.

Although I had time on my hands while I was in bed, there didn't seem to be enough time to do everything. I read a lot and I had a large amount of mail to sort out with Gabrielle White, my secretary. She and her typewriter took a pounding answering all the correspondence. I also watched quite a bit of football on television, and found myself watching the footballers' legs and knees.

I spent hours watching how they worked just to reassure myself that mine were going to work like that. I had to think positively and direct my efforts to getting better.

There were endless comings and goings with visitors and I never became bored. Samantha was only four and a half years old and when she heard I'd broken my legs she thought it was like her doll. When her doll's legs were broken, they came off – and she was concerned that this must have happened to mine. When she came to see me the first thing she did was to remove the bedclothes. All she saw was the plaster, of course. She could see the tops of my legs going into the plaster – but there was no way of her knowing that my legs were there. When she took a closer look she saw a little square hole in each plaster. The nurses had cut them to put in metal plates to give my legs electric shocks to keep the muscles moving as the nerves were still damaged. Samantha kept putting her fingers through those little holes, without saying anything, just to see if my legs were still there.

The sisters and nurses were marvellous. They tried to keep the press and television people away at first but I told them that I liked them around. I was pleased they were taking an interest in me as, from my point of view, I was just an ordinary person who happened to be in hospital because my legs weren't right. Their visits kept me in touch with the outside world and I enjoyed them coming.

The nursing staff were all part of a team and so was I. There were no divisions at all, we were like one large family and we all worked together at getting me better. It reminded me of my rowing days. They were doing all they could and it was up to me to make sure I did everything I could to get myself fit as quickly as possible. The only time I ever crossed swords with one of the sisters was over the length of my hair, which she disapproved of. I did ask the barber to call once. When sister came in she pretended to faint at the sight of me with a towel round my shoulders having my hair cut.

I was doing a fair amount of physiotherapy and was

always asking the doctors what sort of progress I was
making. I'd will the toes of each foot to pick up something
off the floor but they just wouldn't work. They told me it
was due to nerve damage but this was something I
couldn't understand. Things did improve gradually with
each week – but there was still intense pain. The only way
to overcome that was to keep my outside interests going
and, after about six weeks, I asked if I could go to a BBC
studio to commentate a race. The staff were fabulous and
let me go. When they took me out of the hospital I
remember looking up at the sky and thinking how marvellous it was to see the clouds rolling by instead of a
static ceiling.

My wheelchair was put in a truck, facing backwards,
so that I could look out of the rear window. As we set
off I thought there was a lunatic at the wheel. We seemed
to be going at a fantastic speed. When I complained, the
driver shouted back that we were only doing 30 m.p.h.
Moving about again at any speed faster than a wheelchair
took quite a bit of getting used to – so I concentrated on
looking at people's legs, especially the girls. I didn't have
much luck; most of them were wearing maxis, a fashion
which had hit the scene while I was in hospital and I'd got
used to seeing nurses in their traditional-length skirts.
I was still keen to see how legs worked and it was a bit of a
disappointment having to watch the mens' legs, instead, as
we drove along.

After commentating the race I went on to a Lotus ball
that evening. It was great fun even though I began to feel
a bit pooped by then. I got out of hospital quite a few
times to go to functions after that. I was supposed to be
back before 9 p.m. when they shut the doors. The sisters
were great sports and I gather they never asked the night
nurses what time I came in. I got to know as many back-
ways into the hospital as any junior nurse. On one
occasion a friend was pushing my wheelchair through an
underground boiler-room at 2 a.m. when we suddenly
found our path blocked by a nightwatchman. I tried to
explain I wanted to come in and when he got over his

surprise at seeing a patient arriving in the middle of the night in a dinner-jacket he said: 'Are they expecting you?'

'I hope so,' I said, 'I live here,' and he finally agreed to let us pass.

I'd never thought about the problems of people in wheelchairs until I went out to these functions. You're terribly captive and when you want to speak to people you find yourself addressing their navel. Some embarrass you by bending or kneeling down, while others elect to stand *behind* you for some reason. You have to carry on the conversation without seeing them. As the evenings wore on I found more and more people did this. They'd say hello as they stood in front, then they'd creep further and further behind you to continue the conversation. I never understood why, unless they didn't like the look of my face.

It's even more embarrassing when you want to go to the loo. They seldom hear you the first time and then you have to shout it. I got quite an insight into the difficulties disabled people have to face. Trying to be social can be pretty tiring when you're in a wheelchair – even though you're sitting down all the time. But I'm sure all of them, like me, wish to be treated as normal people.

Apart from the outside events I was attending, everything was built around my physiotherapy. When they took me to the hospital's stationary bicycle for exercise for the first time I did the prescribed fifteen minutes work-out and then they took me back to bed. When the nurses left the room I got out of bed into the chair and wheeled myself back to the exercise room for another session on the bicycle. I was determined to walk and return to racing as soon as possible and the only way to achieve that was to step up my series of leg exercises. This was something positive and I really felt I was beginning to get somewhere at last.

I talked them into letting me go out one Saturday, telling them I had some important things to attend to. I got my driver to take me down to Kent where Bette and I had a cottage. I'd organized things beforehand very secretly so that a Land Rover would be waiting for me with a special seat. It was a swivel seat, a typist's chair in fact, fixed to the rear of an open Land Rover. When we arrived I was lifted out of the car and plonked on the seat and off I went for a day's shooting. This is one of my favourite sports and it was great to be out in the open country all day even though it was freezing cold and raining. When I got back to the hospital that evening it seemed ludicrous to have spent all day driving around in a Land Rover shooting game – and then to come back and have the nurses taking care of me, undressing and putting me in bed, like an invalid again.

I was allowed home for an occasional Sunday. It was super to be with my family again in the home surroundings. When I arrived in the wheelchair Samantha took the blanket off to check that my legs were still there. It must have been a horrible time for her when one realizes she needed this reassurance so constantly.

My visits, especially when I was allowed home for a whole week-end, put a big extra load on everyone and Bette in particular. In hospital they do everything for you and know exactly how to deal with things as the whole of the treatment is geared to caring for the patient. But when you come home you suddenly realize what a bloody nuisance you are. The family have to fetch, carry and move everything for you. Even shaving was quite an operation with everything having to be brought to me. I'm sure I wore everyone out. I wasn't allowed to put any weight on my legs and I had to be lifted on to the bed Bette had made up in the sitting-room. My feet still couldn't support themselves and they had to have a mass of pillows under and between them. Damon had a fine old time when I was on the bed because he took over my wheelchair and dashed about the house using it as a sort of prototype racing car. After he'd done a few laps there was hardly any paint left in the hall.

Before I came out of hospital for good we had quite a party. It was just before Christmas and they let the nurses off the lead a bit. Sister wasn't too keen on my saying much about it because she thought her senior nursing officers might not approve if they knew all that happened. It was a super party so, perhaps, we'd better leave it at that. I had tremendous treatment in hospital and they did a fabulous job.

The children were a bit apprehensive when I arrived home. One of the first things they did was to bring me their school reports. They wanted to get the worst bit over so we could all settle down and enjoy Christmas. I always read their reports with them and go through each item to see how they've made out. If they haven't done so well I like to find out why. If they've done well I praise them. I hated having my reports read, but it seems that each generation inflicts this ritual on the next. Like all parents I feel elated when they've done well.

9
Race against Time

Flying has always been one of my great joys and when I returned home, after being in hospital for almost three months, one of my targets was to get my pilot's licence back. Getting in and out of my plane was a problem as I was still hobbling around on sticks. The flying part was easy. It's always easier to do things if you've got to and, around this time, I was asked to go to a home for crippled children. I was able to drive my car – that's one of the things I had very little trouble with – but it would have been a long journey so I decided to fly.

When I arrived I wished I'd gone by car. I had one hell of an effort getting out of the plane and down the wing and I had to do it in front of all these crippled children. I was supposed to be a sort of 'before and after' example – and yet, there I was gritting my teeth barely able to walk. Every step was agony but I knew I just had to get the message across to those children or they'd lose hope and become even less mobile themselves. When I got close to them I was still gritting my teeth, but it's possible to do this and make it look as though you are smiling. The smiles they gave me back were tremendous and by the time I had left I wasn't sure who was supposed to be inspiring who but I know I felt a lot better after meeting them.

The South African Grand Prix was only a couple of months away and I was going along, at that time, to the Royal National Orthopaedic Hospital at Stanmore each morning to receive treatment for my legs. The three-hour sessions were spent riding a static exercise-bicycle in the gym, some swimming in the pool and work on a bench with weights on my legs.

I drove the four miles each way from my home at Mill Hill at first, then I started to do the journey on a push-bike. This was because the doctor at Stanmore had said he saw no prospect of my driving a racing car with any degree of competence for at least another six to nine months. He told me there was still very significant damage to important nerves around both knees which control the power of the feet. I'd made up my mind I was going to drive in the South African Grand Prix and riding a bicycle to and from my therapy, as well as riding a stationary one while there, seemed to me the only way to regain knee movement and build up leg muscle to achieve this target.

The treatment I received was exactly the same as any other patient with comparable leg injuries, and I had every confidence in my doctor who was always perfectly honest about my condition and progress.

When I was on the bicycle in the gym I never spoke to anyone, the patients, doctor or staff. This was the most important race of my life – even though the bloody bicycle was fixed to the floor. I had to get through the quota of exercises I'd set myself over and above that laid down by the hospital. I used to be pretty bushed when I got home but Bette was always there, backing me up, and she was great.

After I had kept this up for some while my legs were still terribly weak and I could barely lift my right leg. They had told me at the hospital that no matter how much exercise I did on my legs, the greatest healer of nerve damage was time. With the Grand Prix now only a month away, time was of the essence and I was very short of essence!

The hospital staff had been marvellous but they thought that I was bonkers. So it became a race against time and their ideas. When I had come home for good from the first hospital I was on crutches. Then I was able to swap them for two sticks, and now I had one. That surely spelt progress but I had to think seriously about this Grand Prix. Obviously, I wouldn't be 100 per cent fit and another problem was that I wouldn't be able to test myself or the car until I got to South Africa. The cars had to go by boat a month before the race and my car had already left England along with the others.

I had signed with Rob Walker's team while I was still in hospital and Colin and I had agreed to go our separate ways. The Lotus Team was dynamic with Colin running it and I enjoyed driving for him; but I'd been with them for three years, and with BRM for seven years, both of which I think are reasonable times. So when Rob Walker asked me to join his team I thought it was a good proposition. I wouldn't be moving too far away as I'd be driving another Lotus anyway.

If I wasn't fit in time and couldn't work or drive the car properly I'd probably be a bit of a menace to myself as well as others, and I wouldn't be able to put up a quality performance. So I would have to go out to South Africa first to give it a whirl in practice before I could make a decision whether to drive or not.

The 1970 season looked like being a very exciting one. All the manufacturers were producing new cars and a lot of the drivers had changed teams. So all the cards had been reshuffled with everyone having new hands, as it were, and this might well upset the form. Some teams would get their new cars sorted quicker than others and as far as I could see this would set the pattern for the first few races. Lots of people wondered if I was doing the right thing. They thought I should have retired after my accident, and the press boys kept asking me why it was so important to get myself ready in time for the South African Grand Prix.

I was very happy to be driving a Lotus. Rob Walker had been a great friend of mine for many years and he was a very successful entrant. I didn't want to stay an invalid. I enjoyed motor racing and just wanted to get back to doing the thing I enjoyed. So it's hardly surprising that I put a bit of an effort into getting ready in time.

I was still a bit wobbly on my pins when I arrived in South Africa. From a medical point of view I was supposed to be out there recuperating and watching the race. I used a bicycle to ride up to the circuit and keep myself in trim, and on practice day, Rob Walker said I could sit in the car and have a go. After I'd put on my gear and they had lifted me in I drove off. I took it fairly gently for the first few laps to settle in and I knew Rob wasn't expecting competitive lap times. In fact, he expected me to stop after having a short drive round, as he had another driver standing by to take over when I came into the pits.

They must have been out of their tiny minds to think that I was going to stop once I'd got in the car. I was really enjoying it. As I gathered speed going along the very long straight there I remember thinking, 'I hope the brakes work.' I found myself just easing my left foot across and tapping the brake pedals, just to check that the pressure was there. That was the only qualm I had – because the straight was long and it gave me a bit of time to think about it. Both feet were still terribly weak and I wasn't able to press on the brakes hard, but they were working and that was something. I was a lot less frightened than I thought I might be. In fact I was amazed how easy it was. I even managed to put in some fast laps, reaching speeds of 170 m.p.h. before my practice was over. I didn't think about a tyre coming off again as it had in America – and I don't know if I was fortunate or stupid, it depends on which way you look at it. I think it is nature's way to make you forget; and that's why we all manage to keep going despite all the things that happen to us.

On race day, my legs were still giving a lot of pain and as I set off I wasn't even sure I could complete the race. I'd been out of action for five months, almost to the day, and you need strength to drive racing cars. About halfway through the race I was hoping I was going to be able to continue. Then I began to drive faster and faster and I finished in sixth place, earning one Championship point. It was a fair reward for all the hours I'd spent on that bloody bicycle.

When I came into the pits it was fabulous to see the pleasure on everyone's faces. They all seemed to share the joy I'd felt that day. It was a great emotional experience. It was a hot day and I'd finished in good order – but my legs didn't feel so hot when I stood up on them. Bette had been in the pits throughout the race with stopwatch in hand. Both of us would have been content if I had just finished the race, but when I came sixth she was as happy as if I'd won.

When I got home there were masses of congratulatory letters and amongst them was one from the sisters and nursing staff at University College Hospital. That really pleased me. I thought it was terrific. Everyone there, and in the hospital in America, and at Stanmore had done a wonderful job. If they hadn't I would never have made that race. My surgeon thought it was too early for me to be aiming to drive in the South African Grand Prix and that I wasn't being fair to myself. He felt so strongly about it that he called round at my home one evening and told Bette so. He said I was perfectly capable of driving, but that the requirements of racing driving demanded a first-class physical and mental state. In his opinion my physical state wasn't good enough and I wouldn't have the reserve that all the other drivers could call on. From a medical point of view he was absolutely right and he had brought round X-rays of my legs to prove it.

I continued my treatment at Stanmore within a couple of days of returning from South Africa and the whole staff were every bit as delighted as I was that I'd made it in that race. That one Championship point was the hardest I'd ever won.

After the accident, Bette and I both began to realize that life was more precious. Something like this puts all the trivial things into proportion. It became even more important to make the most of every minute and moment. There were lots of things I wanted to do and I didn't want to be doing them in six months time. I wanted to be doing them now. My ambition was to win every race I entered, and live to be a hundred.

I get a lot of pleasure from racing and when the flag drops, everything I've got goes into winning that race. It's my way of life and has been for many years. When the race is on it's still one man in his machine against all the others. Racing is a way of fulfilling a role in life. It enables me to come to terms with myself, to know what sort of person I am.

All drivers know fear and when we come face to face with it we have to overcome it. If I thought I was going to be killed motor racing I'd be bloody stupid to do it. Obviously, I had confidence in my own ability otherwise I wouldn't have wanted to continue. Everyone takes risks. On ordinary roads throughout the world the toll of people being killed or injured is appalling. Whenever you drive or walk on the roads you're taking a risk. You're aware of the dangers, like everyone else, but it doesn't stop you continuing to be a driver or pedestrian. You take precautions and you hope it won't happen to you. Anyone who doesn't think that and have hope would be a bit of a nut.

Admittedly, we're sticking our necks out a bit further in racing, but I enjoy driving – on the roads and motor racing. I enjoy driving go-karts too but, without doubt, Formula 1 driving has given me the most pleasure and satisfaction of all classes of racing because it's the highest form of motor racing and, consequently, much more difficult. It's more competitive and if you do well you get a greater sense of achievement.

Many people think that racing drivers are fearless, but they're not; if they were, they'd be a menace to themselves and to the other drivers. If we didn't know fear we wouldn't last very long, and I'm sure this works as a sort of safety valve which helps keep the old self-preservation thought well to the fore, which is terribly important. Although fear does play a part in racing driving – you've got to devise some means of overcoming it. It's a challenge

9. Jimmy and I got a tremendous reception at London
Airport – and from Bette, Damon and Brigitte – after Indy.

TOP OPPOSITE   11. Gipsy children came along for the ride during filming of *Caravan to Vaccares*. They were terrific.

BOTTOM OPPOSITE   12. A very happy evening. Prince Charles jokes with Bette before the Lord's Taverners Silver Jubilee Ball. October 1975.

ABOVE   10. The Duke of Edinburgh, President of the British Racing Drivers' Club, having a look at the Embassy I work from.

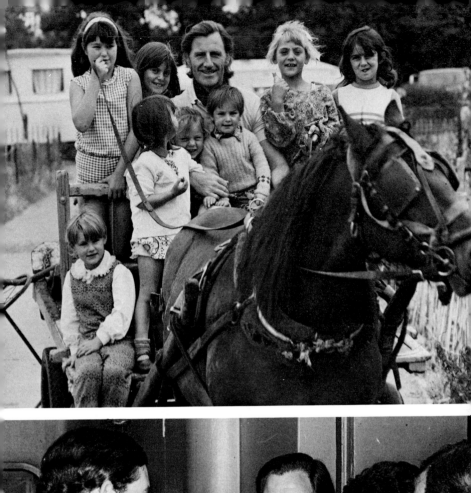

ABOVE 13. Two Champs. The one on the right is David Broome's and bit me shortly afterwards.
BELOW 15. Damn dangerous this cricket!

ABOVE 14. When I retired I was so busy I had to turn down shooting days. For me, this was unheard of.
BELOW 16. I'm not much good at fishing as the evidence shows – but I love it just the same.

really. Learning to control yourself as well as the car and then trying to do it better than your competitors.

When Bette gave me an address book in 1954, the year before we were married, it was only intended to be a small present – but it's something I've carried with me ever since. It has a whole lot of addresses in it, of course, and also the punch lines for quite a few jokes. It also contains this definition of fear and panic:

> *Fear is the first time you find you car'*
> *do something for the second time.*
> *Panic is the second time you find you can't*
> *do it for the first time.*

The thing that frightens most people, in any walk of life, is fear of the unknown. Whenever I got into a racing car I had to have confidence in my own ability and that of the designer to design the car correctly and the mechanics to bolt it together properly; and I had to have confidence in my fellow drivers, when driving close alongside them, that they weren't going to make mistakes.

Even so – like all other drivers I realized that things can go wrong and the unexpected can happen and that it could be dangerous. When you come round a very fast corner, for instance, and suddenly see a patch of oil on the track – that can be frightening. It's the same if you spin off. But you're so busy allowing for the oil and correcting for it and trying to control any skid that you might get into – that it isn't until afterwards you feel the fear. Then your legs might feel like bars of milk or something; but the type of fear you feel at the time is when you have to go fast in the wet. Even when there's only a thin layer of water on the track the wide 'dry' treadless tyres can aquaplane – and that's very frightening indeed. The tyres just get on top of the water like a boat, or water-ski, and you have no control over the car.

When I was driving in the Le Mans 24-hour endurance race some years before, I had just come through the pit area with everything in bright sunshine – and then when I was going along the fastest bit of the track along the

Mulsanne straight there was a cloud-burst. When you're steaming along in the wet at around 200 m.p.h. and you're on 'dry' tyres – it's very tippy-toey! When the car goes out of control there's nothing you can do. You just have to sit there and not do anything until it sorts itself out, and you just hope there's not a corner coming up. The water gets on the screen, too, and you can't see properly. You're looking through water, everything's distorted and it's difficult to judge where the kerbs are.

I was frightened at Le Mans on another occasion when it wasn't raining – *at night*. There's a kink in the Mulsanne straight just over the brow of the hill and you can't see it. As you go hurtling down it there's a 100-yard board to warn you; but as you go over the top of this hump your lights are pointing up in the sky, just when you're wanting to look down at the road to see where the apex of the corner is. You can't quite see it, and you've got to take it flat out. You have to be pretty accurate and I got to the point where I was counting. As I went past the signpost I'd start counting 'one . . . two . . . three . . . four, TURN' – and that's how I turned that corner at night. It worked – but you've got to be able to count . . . regularly!

Very often one fright can cancel out another – as a more desperate situation presents itself. Then you're so busy trying to put both things right that you haven't time to be afraid.

Fear is nature's early warning system to safeguard self-preservation and I think the greatest fears come when you are comparatively new to anything. When I competed in the Belgian Grand Prix at Spa for the first time in 1958 – I almost quit. It's one of the fastest tracks in the world and during the practice I was so scared – I returned to the pits. Then I remembered my early struggles to get even this far up the motor racing ladder. I got back into the car and set off round the track a little more slowly at first to play myself back in – and then increased the speed up to the point where I had been scared before. Then I pushed it beyond that. I felt better and at the end of the practice session I had no problem.

That was when I was pretty new to the sport. Since then I know I'd be more frightened of the reactions from the people in the pits if I came in and said I was stopping because I didn't fancy it.

One does meet some horrible situations though, particularly when you come across the wreckage of a 'shunt' which you know the driver couldn't have escaped from. These sort of accidents are more often than not due to mechanical failure – seldom driver's error. The engines, chassis, wheels and tyres have tremendous demands made on them in Grand Prix racing and things do go wrong, break up and fall off. Then it can be frightening. You don't know if and when it's going to happen – so in a way we're back to the fear of the unknown.

Each driver knows the other drivers are having this same sort of problem and because the stakes are so high in motor racing, we have to take risks. But they're calculated and we know what we're doing. At least I hope we do. When we take a risk we make sure it's worth the gamble – and we hope we will be doing it better than anybody else. You have to have hope in this life, otherwise there'd be no point in getting out of bed in the morning.

Each circuit has its own problems and this variety makes racing the more exciting. The whole essence of motor racing is to overcome the problems and do it that much better than your competitors. The actual sensation of controlling a racing car on a circuit and expressing myself through a machine gives me a lot of pleasure. Man has always been in some sort of danger ever since he first set foot on earth. It certainly gets the old adrenalin going. I think people who experience danger tend to place a higher value on life itself. They put more into life and get more out.

I try never to look back, except in a driving mirror. I have emotions, like everyone else, and I've felt them many times on the track. I try not to let them show, particularly if I haven't done too well. If I allowed myself to get too upset with a poor performance in one race I would be unlikely to approach the next in the right frame of mind.

I get tremendous pleasure from having done well and, if I've won, well that's a bonus.

The biggest bonus of all is taking part in a sport I enjoy . . . and getting paid for it. I think it's terribly important for every man and woman to work at something they enjoy doing. Unfortunately, life being what it is, not everyone achieves this fulfilment. Many people do unglamorous jobs extremely well, day in and day out, without anyone ever noticing their contribution to life. In motor racing we're particularly fortunate because we receive recognition – and even greater acclaim when we do well.

As I said before – man is a competitive animal and he can't just switch it on and off. We all want to do well – and we need to experience danger to overcome our fears so as we can do well. I think man maintains a better balance if he experiences danger every now and again. It titillates him and makes him more aware of being alive.

I have a lot of respect for people who put their neck on the line. My admiration for the chaps who climb Everest and do similar things is boundless – and I feel the same way about my competitors in motor racing.

It never occurred to me that I was being unfair to my family by earning my living in such a dangerous way. Bette has always gone along with my motor racing even before we were married. She has never tried to stop me or even said anything that would, in effect, mean that she didn't like it. She's been apprehensive, of course, like any other woman would be. Whether the children are apprehensive I wouldn't know. If my family had wanted me to stop racing, I would have been a very unhappy man, miserable and probably unbearable. My family bene-fited from my racing and their whole way of life would have been different without it, and if I'd given it up after my accident in America – who knows, I could have gone to the dogs – and that wouldn't have been fair to my family.

10

The Will to Win

Prince Charles' love of adventure is well known and he wanted to try his hand at driving a racing car round the Thruxton circuit, so I lent him mine. Off he went in the Formula 2 single-seater and I was supposed to tail him in an Aston Martin. His car was capable of 160 m.p.h. and I think he must have been trying to reach it because he left me on the first bend. As I chased after him it started to rain. He was on smooth dry-weather tyres and I thought he might crash. I put my foot down to try an catch him and as I came round the bend, I saw him spinning. I thought: 'Crikey – he's the heir to the throne . . . If he crashes, I'll be the heir to the Bloody Tower.' It was a hair-raising moment but he managed to stay on the track, thank goodness.

I've played cricket a few times with him and he's certainly better at the game than I am. I can't run (never could) for a start, and that's a bit of a handicap. It's also one of the reasons why I took up a sport where I could take part sitting down. I often played cricket in teams of racing drivers for various charities. They were always good fun – though the spectators were often amazed when they saw us in action. Some of us are terrified of that little cricket ball. Quite rightly, too, it's hard and just look what it can do to you. To outsiders it may seem a far less dangerous game than Grand Prix driving, but from where I find myself standing when I'm batting it doesn't seem like that at all.

It all boils down to confidence in one's ability. When the ball comes down like an express train I don't quite know what to do about it. I experience a fear of the unknown – well, maybe that's not quite true, because I've got a pretty good idea of what it's going to do to me and I don't fancy it. I lack the confidence in my ability to deal with it.

It's the same with that other sport which takes place on four legs. I wouldn't fancy going round Tattenham Corner on a horse at around 40 m.p.h. You can't control it, at least I can't, and it's got a mind of its own. You're too far from the ground for one thing. David Broome and I changed horsepower for a giggle once. He found it a bit odd having to drive a racing car almost lying down, and I soon had confirmation that you never know what a horse might do at any given moment. I like horses and I used to ride a bit when I was a boy. It was obviously a right decision to jack it in because David Broome's horse bit me!

I felt far more at home playing golf and my interest in it was awakened after my accident. I was still working to strengthen my legs and my doctor told me that one of the best ways of doing this was to walk a lot. Up until then I'd knocked a ball around the golf course and all that I knew of the game came from reading a couple of books. If I was going to follow the medical advice and walk four miles a day it seemed sensible to enjoy it and do it on the golf course. I was hooked on the game before, though I had little time to play, and I became even more hooked now, particularly after I'd had half a dozen lessons from a professional.

Golf, in a way, demands the same mental approach as motor racing. You need concentration, self-control, judgement, co-ordination, good reactions, timing and rhythm. When you come to think of it, those same qualities are needed for good everyday motoring on the roads. One of the great things about golf is that a rabbit can always play with an expert, and if he is playing somewhere near his handicap he can have a good game. I don't think that applies to any other sport.

I had some very enjoyable games of golf with Douglas Bader. He never, ever, gave up when he lost both legs in an air crash. He kept himself superbly fit and his shoulders and arms were like steel. Just to play alongside him had a therapeutic effect.

I always tried to fit in some golf whenever I travelled to a motor race abroad, but my racing went through a bad patch in the 1970 season. After coming sixth in the South African Grand Prix I finished in the same position in the British Grand Prix, fifth at Monaco, and fourth in the Spanish. That wasn't too good but the most tragic thing of all was the loss of three very good friends: Bruce McLaren, Piers Courage, and my former Lotus team-mate, Jochen Rindt.

Bruce McLaren was killed testing his car at Goodwood. Piers Courage died when his car overturned and caught fire in the Dutch Grand Prix – and Jochen Rindt won five Grands Prix . . . Monaco, the Dutch, French, British, and German . . . before being killed during practice for the Italian Grand Prix. Although there were still three more Championship races to go, he had five more championship points than the nearest rival at the end of the season and became the first posthumous World Champion.

The Monaco Grand Prix was the first that Jochen Rindt won that season. I was glad he had; and I was pleased, too, that my fifth place had taken me past the long-standing record of the number of World Championship points that Fangio held until then.

The driving force behind every successful racing driver is the will to win. Any athlete, sportsman or anyone who takes part in something competitively must have this will to win. It covers a whole load of things such as determination, improving oneself and striving for perfection all the time. What you're trying to do, basically, is beat the next man. It all adds up to competitive spirit. I don't know whether it's in-born or come-by, but I think there has to be something there initially – a combination of factors that make you want to prove yourself and rise above your fellows. Man is a competitive animal and the will to win is everything.

There's not much satisfaction in winning a motor race when other drivers have dropped out through mechanical failures. That takes the edge off it. The real pleasure comes from beating everyone in the race – and this starts with the practice sessions. Even if you are the only car on the track during practice you're still competing with all the other drivers by striving to put in the fastest lap to get the pole position on the grid. This gives you an advantage at the start of the race as the track is clear ahead and you don't have to plough your way through the rest of the field. Sometimes you or your car can go badly in practice and you find yourself at the rear of the grid. Whenever I found myself in this position I didn't give in. You kid yourself that you meet a better class of person back there, and then remind yourself that no race is won until somebody has crossed the finishing line and got the chequered flag. You never know – it could be you.

So during the practice you're not only trying to do better than the other drivers: you're competing with yourself in trying to improve on your performance and achieve the perfect lap. Nothing's perfect in this world and its unlikely that you will ever put in the perfect lap; but you keep trying all the same. To succeed, you've got to go fast and the only way you can go fast, consistently, is to take the corners properly and so get your car through all the corners and around the circuit in the minimum time. During the practice you might have braked a little too soon for a corner, losing a fraction of a second. So next time round you go into that corner deeper before you brake. It works and you're delighted – but when you come to one of the corners on the other side of the circuit you make a monkey's of it and lose time on that corner which you took perfectly each time round before. You keep going round, trying to get everything together and all the corners right, pushing yourself and your car on to as near perfect a performance as it is possible to achieve. In doing this you're bound to take risks and go into some corners too fast and this can be just as lethal as if you were driving in a race alongside all the other cars and drivers.

You need to know what you are capable of when you extend yourself. Rowing taught me a lot about myself. It's a sport that requires self-discipline, stamina, strength and fitness for you must go on even when you think there's absolutely no way you can continue. This means you have to force yourself beyond the pain barrier. It's very easy when rowing in an eight for someone to thumb in a few limp ones and take a slight respite. But you can't do this without letting the rest of the crew down and losing the race. Everyone needs to be 100 per cent reliable. During the last quarter of a mile in a hard-fought race you experience acute physical pain. Your body is crying out to stop and there's no way you can put in another stroke – but you must. You know that everyone else in the boat is feeling the same – and so are the rival crew. So you continue to force yourself to do better than your rivals. Rowing taught me never to give in.

In motor racing, this determination has to come to terms with the desire for self-preservation but, always, there must be this will to win. If someone is on my tail and trying to take me on a corner I naturally make it difficult for him. I slam the door on him so he can't pass. If he tries the other side I move over and shut the door again. That's motor racing. He'd do the same to me. You don't deliberately baulk anybody. There's a distinction between legitimate gamesmanship and deliberate baulking. If the bloke on your tail out-drives you in a corner you let him through. But he's got to earn it and prove that he is out-manoeuvring you. You try hard, of course, not to let anybody by. But you don't resort to dirty driving. The sport is pretty clean and there's a very high standard of sportsmanship on the track today.

If there's a driver immediately in front of you it's legitimate to put the pressure on. You bloody well have to. You've got to rattle them and pressure them into making mistakes by getting them to think about you instead of their driving. There's nothing more demoralizing when you're in the lead and someone creeps up on you and gets right on your tail, despite all your efforts. When you're doing your best this situation provides the true test of a Grand Prix driver. It's happened to me often – and I've been responsible for having it happen to other drivers. I've seen them begin to crack under the strain as I piled the pressure on.

I used to adopt the same tactics when I was rowing. If, when I was stroking the London Rowing Club first eight, I saw a member of the other crew make a slight mistake I'd take advantage of it immediately. I'd call for a 'ten' to increase our striking rate and pile on the agony to take an even bigger advantage of their little mistake. Even after we'd gained a foot or two and were continuing to draw away I'd still drive it right home to get the other crew into a losing frame of mind and even more rattled.

You've probably noticed during the Oxford and Cambridge Boat Races that, although both crews race the same distance, the losing crew always flop over their oars at the finishing line and look the most exhausted. When you win a race tiredness just floats away in the elation. It's a question of mind over matter – and it's the same in motor racing. You don't want to pressure all the other drivers to go off the circuit. The big thing is to get by them and as you exert pressure you watch them begin to get a little bit untidy. As the tension increases they start making quick movements instead of smooth ones. You wouldn't be human if this didn't encourage you to take advantage of their errors, seize your chance, and fly on by.

It's good to see them fade back in your mirror. This doesn't happen often, though, as most Grand Prix drivers make a habit of coming back for more. You get to know who these people are likely to be and you know what sort of opposition to expect from the reference library you keep in your mind about the other drivers. As you gain fresh experience with each race you file it away – ready for use during this and future races. It's race

strategy to know what to expect from your opponents –
this is how races are won and lost.

If you're in the lead and you come across a back-marker
tailing the field who doesn't move over and get out of the
way, gives a lot of trouble and holds you up, this can be
extremely annoying. Particularly if the other drivers
you were leading are catching you up and starting to
breathe down your neck. But the one thing you mustn't
do is lose your temper. If you lose control of yourself there
is just no way you are going to control a car. You can get
pretty close to losing your temper at times, but you've
got to watch it and be careful because these are the sort of
situations when you can make a mistake. When people
lose their temper, emotion takes over. It takes charge of
the brain and then they're without reason. You've
noticed it, no doubt, when you're having a discussion with
someone and they've got het-up and lost their temper and
the whole thing degenerates into an argument. Then it's
impossible to reason with them. So we've got to have this
self-control at all times.

I've come pretty close to losing my temper. I nearly did
at the Belgian Grand Prix three years or so before I
retired from racing driving. At the previous Grand Prix
at Monte Carlo my car wouldn't start for the practice
session. I completely missed the whole of the first practice
session, which is vital, and I was a bit brassed off about it.
Then I went to the Belgian Grand Prix – and what
happened? I did one lap and the flipping car stopped out
in the circuit. I was furious. I was really throwing a few
bloody things. If anyone had been around I think they
would have said I'd lost my temper. But I wasn't *in* the car.
If you lose your temper in the car you're in dead trouble.
You'll be unlikely to complete the race in one piece – let
alone win it.

Although there's very strong rivalry between drivers
there's also extremely good camaraderie. We're not
soppy friends but even when we're off the track there's
still this rivalry, a bit of one-upmanship. The only time
you can really relax is if you are completely alone with one

or two of them. Otherwise there's always this intense rivalry. It's necessary because we're in a very competitive sport and you need this competitiveness to do well in it – because you've got this one great big instinct of self-preservation. At the same time, you've got to find out where this fine balance lies – and you've got to know your own fears and you've got to know how to contend with them to achieve this balance.

That race at Monaco in 1970 had a cheering ending for me. As I was sitting on some tyres in the pit I heard someone shout out: 'Hello, Graham.'

When I looked up – it was my surgeon. He had taken the trouble to come all the way on a charter flight to Monte Carlo just to watch the race.

I I

The Triple Crown

As I was walking across Regent Street one day a chap
popped his head out of a drain and said: 'Hiya, Graham.'
Taxi drivers often hail me with a dirty great grin and say:
'Wanna drive it?'

When I took Bette and Brigitte to one of the Alistair
MacLean film premières we were late and couldn't get a
taxi. After standing on the kerb for some while a whole
flock of them came by – all engaged. Then I heard a
voice from one of them in the middle of the road shout out:
''Ere, Graham – hop in, Mate.' When we arrived at the
cinema they were getting ready to receive Princess Anne
and we were supposed to be in the line up inside. As we
shot out of the taxi and I was fumbling for my money –
the driver sensed the urgency and said: 'Okay, Mate –
have it on me,' and drove off into the night.

I never cease to be amazed at the people who recognize
me – particularly abroad. The 1971 season started with
even more exposure. I was at the Hilton Hotel and had
just made the official announcement about signing a
contract with the Brabham team, for the forthcoming
Grand Prix season, to a hundred or so press and television
people – and we came to the questions. These usually go
on for some time but there was something odd about this
occasion. Only a few were asked and then there was an
embarrassing silence. As I looked round the room I
noticed that the three television cameras were not
operating and that seemed odd, too. Then, without

93

warning, all the camera lights went on and in came Eamonn Andrews clutching that famous *This Is Your Life* album. He took me into the next room before I had time to recover. It had been turned into a studio, with an audience already assembled.

I've often wondered how Eamonn manages to maintain the surprise with this programme, but Bette and my friends kept the secret and I hadn't an inkling until the vital moment. My parents joined Bette and me as my past life unfurled. Jack Brabham knew about the programme, but he never dropped the slightest hint. He came in and others followed: Stirling Moss, Tony Rudd from BRM, and Innes Ireland who, incidentally, had originally got me interested in flying. To my utter amazement a voice came over the speaker and in walked my brother – who had flown over from Vancouver. They also flew Jackie Stewart back from South Africa specially for the programme. It was very moving to be confronted so unexpectedly by these and other characters from my past.

Something else happened that year that I never expected and I have a little gavel on a stand at home to commemorate it, which reads: 'Guild of Professional Toastmasters' Award to Graham Hill for the Best After Dinner Speaker in 1971'. I didn't even know I was being considered for this award and, as I was just a racing driver, I was delighted. It was presented at the Guild's annual dinner at the Dorchester in May of the following year. Just before it the press asked me if I could sum up the technique of successful speech-making, in a sentence or two, as this would interest others who have to make speeches themselves. I said I thought it was important to be topical and yet sound spontaneous as though what you were saying had just occurred to you. Make the audience smile or, better still, laugh; and leave them wanting more.

Having said that – what happened? After my speech at the dinner a woman came up to me and said: 'I hope you drive better than you speak.'

She was right. I'd cocked it up and made the worst

speech of my career. It was embarrassing to Bette, to me, and everyone present. I just didn't get with it. The atmosphere and occasion threw me because I knew they were expecting something great. It was rather like going up to a comedian and asking him to make you laugh – just like that. I react to atmospheres and, as speech-maker, it was *my* job to create the right one. But, sub-consciously, I suppose I was over-awed by the occasion and all the famous people who had won the award before me.

I mentioned earlier that I was introduced to flying by Innes Ireland. He used to fly me in his own plane to races in the early days. Quite a few drivers had their own planes, including Jimmy Clark. Everyone got worked up about flying; they were terribly enthusiastic, but I wasn't all that interested at first. However, as it seemed a good way of getting to and from race tracks I eventually took some lessons. Once I did this I got hooked myself, just as I had during my first few laps in a racing car. I got a great feeling of release and independence when I found myself at the controls, leaving the ground. But it was nothing like the satisfaction I felt when I bought my first aircraft with the Indianapolis winnings – or even as great as when I changed that for a six-seat twin-engined Piper Aztec four years later.

I used to fly to race meetings and on business trips all over Europe. It took the strain out of travelling besides giving a great sense of freedom on leaving the earth – rather like a large bird, free to go anywhere. I could fly to the South of France, for instance, comfortably in three and a half hours or so. Even short journeys gave me a lot of pleasure. I could be at Brands Hatch in under fifteen minutes, instead of wasting two hours driving across London and going there by car. Flying was not only more convenient and less tiring, it dovetailed perfectly into motor racing and I enjoyed it so much it became a hobby. The navigation side of it gave me a lot of satisfaction, too, particularly on the longer trips. There's always the problem of the weather – and that needs a lot of respect.

Battling with the elements calls for a great deal of effort and concentration.

I would have loved to have been around in the pioneering days when man first learnt to fly. It must have been a terrific adventure. We don't seem to have anything to fill that space at the moment, or that of the car pioneers. You can go skin-diving or jump out of an aeroplane with a parachute. I took some diving lessons in Portugal but I haven't done any parachuting, and I'd love to do that; but neither of these are new to the world like the pioneering days of flying and motoring. You and I can't go on a moon walk yet. I was absolutely staggered when the American astronauts did this, and thought it the most fascinating and awe-inspiring event that had ever taken place. I stayed up all night to watch it on the box and thought it fantastic.

The first time I ever felt I had got something for nothing was when I went up in a sailplane in America. It was marvellous to be able to stay aloft and just drift and soar without any means of self-propulsion.

Another fabulous experience was when I was invited to fly with the Red Arrows. Their formation looks close, when viewed from the ground, but when you're up there with them – they're really close! As I looked sideways I found myself staring at someone else's wing tip. I looked up at the leader and our nose was right under his tail. There was a *Daily Express* photographer in one of the planes alongside mine and as we went into a particularly difficult manoeuvre he called on the radio: 'Turn towards me, Graham, and smile.' Damn fool! We were doing about 500 m.p.h. and the G-forces were pulling me down in my seat and contorting my face. He got an interesting picture. Then the formation dived towards a Gloucestershire valley and popped up at the last moment for a low-level streak towards their airfield at Kemble. There were several mechanics in front of the hangars and as we whooshed a few feet above them they threw themselves on the ground. It looked hilarious from where I was sitting.

I achieved another ambition round about that time -- the ambition of all learner golfers, I imagine: I went round in under 100, at the Carthage Club in Tunis. I was competing in a match with other sportsmen and show-biz people as guests of the club and I carded 97. I got that down to 92 a few days later, but they still called me 'Iron-man Hill' on account of some rather off-beat iron shots I made.

At the time my home club was Mill Hill but I played in several overseas countries besides Tunis that season, such as Bogota, South Africa, America, France and Germany; also in a £4000 Pro-Am Golf Tournament at the Royal Mid-Surrey at Richmond in aid of the National Society for the Prevention of Cruelty to Children, the National Playing Fields Association and the Golf Foundation. The third of these, incidentally, not only introduces thousands of young people to golf every year, but also provides golf instruction for the physically handicapped. My game isn't as worthy as the causes but, when I'm being watched by crowds, I usually manage to do a Spiro off the first tee.

I didn't do very well in the 1971 Grand Prix season – but was as pleased with coming tenth in the Dutch Grand Prix as I have been when I've won some other races. It was run in the rain and the cars which finished ahead of me were fitted with tyres which were better in the wet than any others. I was fastest of the bunch that weren't fitted with these tyres and that was very satisfying.

There was a close duel with Jackie Stewart during the *Daily Mail* Race of Champions at Brands Hatch. Our cars almost touched at times. I managed to put in the fastest lap of the race but, at the halfway stage, I made many attempts to get past Jackie but couldn't. He came second, with Clay Regazzoni winning the race, and me retiring with engine trouble fifteen laps from home.

About this time the critics thought my career was over, but some weeks later I won the GKN/*Daily Express* International Trophy at Silverstone and I must say everyone seemed delighted with the result. It was my first Formula 1 victory since the shunt in America. Bette and our three children watched the race so it was also a happy family occasion. Peter Gethin took second place and both of us were due to play in a Pro-Am Charity Golf Tournament in Scotland the next day. So I flew him to Glasgow, with Bette. Peter Gethin is one of the best golfers among the Grand Prix drivers and we often play together. He likes to take money off me but says it's not easy because when he's about to drive off, or hole a putt, I tell him his shoelace is undone or give him some other gem of useful information.

Jackie Stewart won six Grands Prix that season, which was hogging it slightly as the record was seven and he became the 1971 World Champion.

In 1972 I met another racer. She had a lovely temperament . . . and four legs. In fact I owned her, or nearly did as I had a half-share in her. She was a chestnut filly trained at Newmarket by Harry Thomson-Jones. When I first met Bought In on the training gallops she was fairly motoring along – after that she seemed to spend most of her time in the pits. She ran three races but never finished in the first six. She kept getting a cough and by the time we finished with her I think she must have had pneumonia.

At the beginning of 1972 we moved from Mill Hill to a larger house in the countryside in Hertfordshire. It had quite a bit of ground with it and as our children were fourteen years, twelve, and seven by now it was an ideal place for them. I was very chuffed when I found the name of the house marked on the Ordnance Survey map. It had quite a history. Some former owners were devoted to music and the arts, and organized many week-end parties for music lovers. Sir Edward Elgar, the greatest English composer of his time, performed some of his own compositions for violin there. He became Master of the King's Musick. Paderewski, the composer and celebrated exponent of Chopin's music, was another regular guest.

Music doesn't mean too much to me, but I am affected by it emotionally. I think we lowered the musical tone a bit when we took over the house, particularly during some of the riotous parties we had there; but we really appreciated the home as a family. Quite often I'd get out of the car in the drive and look across at the house, garden, and fields around it and turn to Bette and say: 'Just look at it. It's *ours*.' I couldn't believe it, it was so lovely!

Golf at that time was still a fascinating but frustrating game for me. Tony Jacklin was a mutual friend of Henry Cooper and myself and we both wanted to play like him. So we went along to John Jacobs at the Sandown Park Golf Centre in Surrey. Our games came on a bundle after lessons from him.

During the summer of 1972 I went to Le Mans for the twenty-four-hour sports car race. I was to co-drive with Henri Pescarolo for the French Matra team. It's essentially an endurance race and one of the most difficult things is to try and contain yourself, particularly at the start. It's not easy for a Grand Prix driver to get into a car and drive the first two hours without actually racing. Everybody wants to lead and nobody likes to be beaten, so you have to exercise self-control and, always, there's the temptation to get in front. It's this rivalry thing again, and the team managers have a job to stop drivers from blowing up their engines in the first couple of hours.

When the initial flush is over and drivers settle down and it's six o'clock in the evening with another twenty-two hours to go, the race gets into a nice old rhythm. It's run on the public highways at speeds well over 200 m.p.h. on certain sections but speed is not everything because, to win this classic, you must still be running at the end.

It's a terrific occasion with the best sports cars coming from factories all over the world and settling into garages all around the city a week before the race. A tremendous amount of testing goes on even before the cars come to Le Mans. I was delighted to be driving for Matra; they were extremely professional and thought of everything down to the minutest detail.

During practice I found it a most enjoyable car to drive. They told me I could rev the engine up and that it would hold for twenty-four hours but I didn't want to

99

risk it. If you're fastest in practice you make the headlines
– but you may not have an engine to race for the start on
Saturday afternoon. Work goes on through the night to
maintain the cars in tip-top condition, with up to 400000
people – the biggest crowd that ever watch a single race –
swarming in from all directions and jostling to get into
every conceivable vantage point. It's really a festival
occasion for the crowd, with bands marching past the pits
and stands, followed by Scouts carrying the flags of all the
competing nations. As the race goes on through the night
and into Sunday morning Mass is celebrated beside the
track along the route.

When the race got under way, the Lola team produced
the strongest challenge. Matra were still insistent that I
could rev the engine without any problems for the whole
twenty-four hours. It was unbelievable. After the initial
challenge from the two-car Lola team the race developed
into a duel between our Matra-Simcas and the three-car
Alfa Romeo team. Although one of our Matras dropped
out on the second lap with a broken engine it didn't
shake our confidence. We kept going hard against the
Alfas and as I used the high revs, as I had been told I
could, my engine continued to go like a d-r-e-a-m!

The team managers hadn't given us any directives
about not racing against ourselves and, as we still had
three Matra-Simcas running, each of us tried to slip in a
few fast laps. As the race developed the rivalry between us
became intense. Everyone in the team wanted to win. I
must say the Matra team that year was the best I've ever
driven for at Le Mans. They were the best prepared team
and put in the most effort. The cars had already completed
the equivalent of two full-length Le Mans races on other
circuits in France, with hours and hours of additional
testing and the team really had produced a fantastic car.
Three hours after the start I was able to take the lead.

Although Le Mans is a classic race which every driver
would like to win, we're not always happy about entering
it. With such a wide speed differential between the fastest
and slowest cars it can be dangerous; but it's a fantastic

race to drive in. You go hurtling along and just watch France go by. We were doing about 220 m.p.h. down the long Mulsanne straight and taking the kink there flat out round the clock. The road isn't all that wide and you get quite a sensation of speed.

When it's four o'clock in the morning and you're cold and tired and doing one of your four-hour stints at the wheel, and you can't see where you're going because it's dark and misty and the rain is coming down, you wonder what the hell you're doing it for. But on Sunday afternoon with only two hours to go, if you're still there, you really start to enjoy it and you're glad you've taken part.

Although it's a long race it's absolutely vital to have very quick pit stops. Seconds wasted can be irritating to the driver. The only way you can get quick stops is to have a good team in the pits and do a lot of practice pit stops before the race.

My car was still pulling the same revs down the 200 m.p.h. straight at the end of the race as it did at the beginning – and we won. This earned me the Triple Crown of motor racing as the first driver to have won the World Championship, Indianapolis and Le Mans.

This was my tenth Le Mans and I was delighted to be in the winning car, of course, but really it was a team effort and I cannot praise my co-driver, Henri Pescarolo, highly enough. We shared the four-hour stints of driving throughout the race, but it was Henri who actually drove the car across the finishing line. This was rightly so – because it was the first victory for a French car there for twenty-two years, with Matra-Simcas taking the first two places. They actually crossed the line together, in formation, although our car finished the 2932 miles race ten laps ahead.

Nothing could stop the French joy at winning the race with an all-French car. The seething mass of excited spectators made it very difficult for Henri and myself to get through to the victory dais.

The whole team received an invitation to lunch with President Pompidou at the Élysée Palace. When he congratulated me on winning I said that I really had no alternative, seeing that it was a French car, with British co-driver – and we were trying to enter the Common Market. We talked through an interpreter and he laughed a lot; then I asked him what he thought of the Channel Tunnel idea? I had some shares and I wanted it straight from the horse's mouth. He gave me a wry smile and said, 'Buying or selling?'

It was good to win – but the victory was marred by great sadness. I didn't hear about it at the time but, with only a third of the race to go, my great friend Jo Bonnier had been killed when his Lola touched another car, shot off the circuit into dense woods, and disintegrated with some of the wreckage thirty feet up in the trees. I'd known Jo since we had driven BRMs together in 1960 – and he, Stirling Moss and I had founded the Grand Prix Driver's Association to help raise the safety standards of the race tracks. Jo was President of the GPDA and worked hard for the sport's safety campaigns. He kept the Association going and many more drivers would have died if it had failed. He had also retired recently from Formula 1 Grand Prix racing – which made his loss all the more ironical.

He was my oldest friend in motor racing and I found it hard to believe he had been killed. I could always have a go at winning another race – but I wouldn't meet Jo again – and the shock detracted enormously from my winning Le Mans. I felt deeply for his wife, Marianne, and two small sons.

When I returned from Le Mans I went straight to an Olympic Appeal Dinner where a racing helmet of mine was to be auctioned for the funds. It was covered with the signatures of fellow Grand Prix drivers and I thought it might, perhaps, fetch a couple of hundred pounds.

It went for £1000; and the chap who bought it wanted to give it to one of his sons who was a spastic child.

12

On and off the Track

After the 1972 Le Mans race I was kept pretty busy with a
full programme of engagements on and off the circuits. I
spent the following week in Beirut where I'd been invited
to look into the possibility of setting up a race track. I
stayed to watch a small car race on the roads and then
flew back to London, arriving about five o'clock – drove
home, changed into a dinner jacket and went to an
official function, getting home about midnight. The next
morning I flew myself north to give a talk to the Man-
chester Luncheon Club. Back to Elstree, home, quick
shower, and to my office in London. I dealt with some
letters with my secretary and then drove off to Guildford.

On the way down I stopped off at my Formula 2
workshop in Cobham and went over a few final details
with the mechanics before they left for Rouen for racing
at the week-end. From Cobham I went to the University
of Surrey at Guildford where I gave a two-hour talk. Next
day, Wednesday, Bette and I flew to Sweden for the Jo
Bonnier funeral, and came back that night. On the
Thursday I flew to Rouen to practise for the Formula 2
race, practised again on Friday and Saturday, and raced
on the Sunday.

I flew back to England on Monday where I had an
invitation to go to Lords to watch the cricket, and on the
same day, would you believe, an invitation to go to
Wimbledon. The original plan was for me to go to Lords
for lunch and Wimbledon for tea, but it didn't turn out

that way. I was wanted that afternoon to record the commentary for a motoring film I had appeared in. That scrubbed my afternoon at Wimbledon but I did sneak in a crafty lunch at Lords. On Tuesday I flew to Italy and practised on Wednesday for a Formula 2 race on Thursday. The calendar was so full I had to race in the middle of the week then. On Friday I flew to Clermont-Ferrand for the French Grand Prix for practice that afternoon. More practice on Saturday, and the race on Sunday.

On Monday I flew to Paris for a press conference organized by Matra for the Le Mans victory. After that, by jet as passenger (which was quite a relaxing change) to Rome for another one, and on to Milan for a third press conference. On Tuesday I went to Germany, on Wednesday to Amsterdam and back to London for yet more press conferences and finally back to Brussels for the last one. On Thursday back to Paris to pick up my plane and fly myself to Austria for a Formula 2 race at the week-end. The next two days were spent in practice, with the race on Sunday; afterwards I flew myself back to England on Monday for the week of the British Grand Prix.

Such pressure may seem hectic but whether it was too much it's hard to say. It's not really a thing you can measure; I think it's a personal thing. If a driver feels it's affecting him he usually lays off one or two races – but it didn't affect me. I may have been a bit irritable occasionally but it's not easy for me to judge. I certainly seemed to spend a lot of time flying.

Perhaps that's why I was once described as a renegade Spitfire pilot who drove a sports car in his spare time. On his show, Michael Parkinson asked if I quibbled with that description and I said I thought I might, if I knew what it meant.

Sometimes I am asked whether I would have been as I am if I hadn't been a racing driver. I don't see how I could have been. I must have been different, obviously, because the things that happen to you in your way of life must have an effect and rub off on you.

Because of exposure on television and in the press I know a lot more people than I might have done in another career. People are more friendly and that must have some effect on me. I can't imagine how anyone can go through life in any activity without it having an effect on them. On the other hand, some people say you never change. I think it would be awful if we didn't.

And names . . . I find them fascinating. Why does everyone's name seem so exactly right for them – and yet they have no personal say in the choice at all? It's a complete lottery.

I'm pleased I got into motor racing. I can't believe I would have had such an enjoyable and exciting life if I had done anything else. But my name, background, and early ambitions had nothing to do with my choosing this career. I just happened to see that advertisement offering trial laps at Brands Hatch – and that was that.

You can't exactly type racing drivers. First I think they're sportsmen – some more than others. Some are also fantastic skiers, tennis players, golfers, swimmers or football enthusiasts. Others don't take part in any sport outside motor racing. Some keep themselves fit playing the games they enjoy; others seem to do it naturally. Line up all the racing drivers from all over the world and you'll find they're as different as chalk from cheese. They all come from different walks of life, look different physically and act differently. There are plenty of tall drivers – but you've got to watch the small ones because short men always seem to get on very well in life. Their lack of inches may provide the challenge that spurs them on to greater efforts than their taller competitors. Napoleon was short and his fighting instinct would probably have made him an excellent racing driver had he been around today.

The one thing that is perhaps foremost among racing drivers is the competitive spirit. The stakes are high and there just isn't room for any pettiness. It may seem that we're living with danger and dicing with death; but what we're really doing is living with a heightened awareness of life. There's a very good spirit – particularly at the meetings of the GPDA I mentioned. We meet at every Grand Prix to discuss safety and decide which race organizers are putting on the finest Grand Prix and which is the safest track, has the best signalling, most efficient marshals and that sort of thing; and at the end of the year we present an award. The meetings are very enjoyable as it's the only chance there is to get together with other drivers because we're usually too busy on the circuit. Unless you happen to be staying in the same hotel – and even then we don't see all that much of each other. At the GPDA meetings there's a lot of camaraderie, joking and larking about and everyone enjoys themselves, and you can feel it in the air. But, at the same time a lot of serious work and discussion is carried out.

Some people think that you can only become good at motor racing if you have the opportunities – but I don't agree. Opportunities don't come along – you make them. I get lots of letters from would-be racing drivers and the first time they refer to my luck I know they are never going to make the grade. You make your own luck. It is a word we all use everyday. I've used it in this book when I've said I'm lucky to be doing the job I enjoy . . . or when I've said I didn't have much luck racing in one season or another. But I don't rely on it to win races. I have to take a tough line because it's a tough game. The luck part might be said to come in if the car doesn't break up on you – but that's not luck. You have some control over which team you drive for and if the cars aren't all that reliable, and keep failing, you do – as a driver – have some say in the matter. If you're leading the race and a wheel falls off, that might be said to be bad luck, but, to me, it's an event that needn't have happened.

Drivers such as Fangio, Moss, Clark and Stewart were natural drivers. I've never been described as this; the commentators have said I had to work at it, and this is true. I had to work hard at it with BRM because, in my view, the car wasn't as good as the Lotus. So obviously it was up to me to do all I could. I don't mind being accused of working at it. I wanted to win and I practised hard until I was quick enough.

Winning is essential to a person like myself, and when Jackie Stewart and I were both racing I wanted to beat him, even if we were in the same team. Whenever I played golf with him I wanted to beat him. I wasn't much good but I still wanted to beat him and he wanted to, and frequently did, beat me. But it didn't suppress my will to win and beat him next time. It's inconceivable to me to do anything just for the sake of doing it. Man is competitive by nature whether he likes it or not and some are more competitive than others.

I think it's easier now to get into motor racing than when I started. There are more motor racing schools and I think they are a very good introduction. They enable you to get into a racing car at relatively little cost and find out for yourself if, in fact, you really want to go racing. Even if you find you're not cut out for it you will have achieved something. You won't go through life wishing you were a racing driver; you will have tried it, then you can divert your energies into something else – something in which, perhaps, you might do very well.

If, on the other hand, you find that motor racing is exactly what you want to do, it will have fired your enthusiasm and you'll make a bigger effort to get into racing. It isn't easy, it needs a lot of determination but if it's really what you want – you'll find a way. What you have to realize is that nobody, necessarily, is going to help you. It's no good hoping that someone will pluck you out of the crowd, put you in a racing car, and make you a racing driver. It just won't happen that way. Everybody is so busy doing something for themselves that they're not going to spend time and effort to put a novice into a racing car. Once you realize that you are on your own, you're already one step up the ladder and on the way to making your own opportunities and getting there purely on your own efforts.

That sounds rather like a lecture – I'm sorry. I know you don't all want to become racing drivers, but I get so many letters from people asking me how they can get into racing that I feel it should be included. The mere fact that there are many more racing cars in existence today must mean there's a greater chance of these people getting their backside into one.

Don't be put off if you haven't got money, or access to it. I started with nothing, didn't know anybody and didn't have a car until I bartered my services as a mechanic to owners in return for drives. Nowadays racing is on a much larger scale with more support from many big firms in it for advertising purposes and, therefore, there's more demand for promising young drivers. But I'm not suggesting it's easy. Only a relatively few manage to make a living out of it and to do really well you've got to climb into the top twenty. Even if you've got money, it doesn't follow that you'll be a great driver.

There are several ways of coming into the sport. Stirling Moss drove a car at an age when most boys are still learning to ride a bicycle. Emerson Fittipaldi started on go-karts as a boy and then went from saloon cars into single-seaters. His success came incredibly fast and he became World Champion at twenty-five. This made him a hero with every young male in Brazil. Ronnie Peterson and Tony Brise were ex-kart champions, too.

I was twenty-four before I drove a car and didn't get a regular drive in a racing car until I was twenty-nine. It's better to start younger and it's not a bad thing to get club experience first, and then try a few rallies and hill climbs and some circuit racing in saloon cars. There is no specific way of getting into racing. If you study each Grand Prix driver you'll find they all managed it in different ways.

Some took well-paid jobs, such as labourers on construction sites for a while, so that they could save up enough money to get into the game, while others, today, are doing so through the Midget Grand Prix Club. Stirling Moss and I have given our support to this branch of motor sport as it's an excellent way for people to start racing, and learn the tactics and techniques involved, at a level most can afford. The midget cars, capable of over 80 m.p.h. are scaled down single-seaters, powered by 1300 c.c. engines, and they run on wide Formula 2-type tyres. The races are contested on quarter-mile oval tracks throughout the country with entries of up to forty cars.

Cliff Davis, who is Vice-Chairman of the British Racing and Sports Car Club, is a midget racing fan and he says: 'A chap can pick up a second-hand racer for about £200 to £300 and start racing. Even the best cars only cost £1000 – while £500 is sufficient to get a good car with a chance of winning.' Stirling Moss says that midget car racing could easily produce a future Formula 1 Grand Prix Champion, and I agree with him.

It helps to have some technical knowledge when you get on to the bigger cars – but it's quite possible to get by without so long as you understand the corrections necessary for setting up your car and can give a reasonable account of any problems to those who have to make the adjustments. But you must have the will to win – and when you lose you must overcome your disappointment and be ready to go out next time with even more determination to win.

You have to learn to be a good loser. I've had all sorts of disappointments. One of the oldest motor races in the world is the Targa Florio in Sicily. I've never won it but Stirling Moss and I nearly did on one occasion. We had a big lead and then, suddenly, a bolt came loose in the back axle and the oil ran out and stopped us three kilometres from the end. That was pretty infuriating.

I've never won the Belgian Grand Prix, either, but I would have won it once if I hadn't run out of fuel. The fuel was in there but it wouldn't transfer itself from one tank to another and the car stopped while in the lead with only about three miles to go.

In one of the French Grands Prix I was leading the race when someone ran into the back of me as I was braking at the end of a very wide straight for a hairpin and spun me round like a top. The engine stopped so I tried to get it going again on the starter. It didn't want to fire and while I was going through all the agony of trying to get it going – the poor driver who had run into me came over looking as though he was going to burst into tears. As I looked across to his car, standing there rather sadly on the side of the road with steam pouring out, it looked as though it was crying too. I wasn't particularly interested in the driver and I must have been wearing one of my scowls because he sort of backed away.

After getting my engine going and setting off I got back into the lead again and pulled ahead of Dan Gurney by about twenty seconds – holding him more or less with the race in my pocket. Then a little pin, the size of a match-stick and worth a penny, broke and the fuel injection wouldn't operate. Dan Gurney won the race and I finally limped home in ninth place.

I did win the World Championship that year so I can't complain. But I lost the whole World Championship in 1964, one of the years when I was runner-up, through another driver making a mistake and running into me during the final Championship race in Mexico. You could say it was bad luck – but I suppose you could say I shouldn't have been there at that particular spot at that precise moment. However, I was there and he was trying to overtake me in a hairpin. He'd had a couple of goes at it, but the last time he just overcooked it – went out of control and thumped me. It bent my exhaust pipes up and I had to come into the pits. I lost so much time that I finished well down in the race – which was won by Surtees with a one point lead.

That was that. It had happened and nothing I could do or say would alter it. That's the way I tend to see things when they have gone wrong. There's no point in worrying about it, or all the other things that happened time and time again to rob me of winning races. I don't look back and, this way, I have few regrets. Hopefully, I learn from these setbacks but I apply them forwards. Basically, if you look forward things tend to get better. Because we all live in hope and if there's no hope there's no life and no point in living.

That's all very well, you may say, but how do you cope when five things go wrong on the trot one after the other? This makes me more determined. It has a positive effect on me to get after it. It all comes back to not giving in. The worse things get, the harder I try.

After I'd given a talk to an audience of young male students once I invited questions and one chap immediately leapt to his feet and asked if I had got into racing as a good way of pulling in the birds. I had to wait for about three minutes while that 200-strong male audience laughed their heads off – and by then, when the roar had died down, all I could say was: 'Bloody h-e-l-l!'

All I will say now, to put the record straight, is that I already had a bird when I started racing – Bette. Perhaps I'd better follow that up with some sort of a reference. One of the few women journalists to work on the Grand Prix circuits, and an excellent one at that, is American Mary Schnall Heglar, and she lives with her husband, Rodger, and family near San Francisco overlooking the Pacific – and this is what she had to say on this question in her book *The Grand Prix Champions*: 'Females of astonishing ages and hopes flock around Graham Hill, and he flirts outrageously with all of them. He has a fine eye indeed – but many a hopeful beauty has failed to take seriously the inalterable fact that Graham is very much a family man. He may be a jaunty devil around the circuits, and he may not wear the leash that some drivers do, but his attractive and spirited wife, Bette, is very much his one woman!'

After that commercial I must admit that I think a variety of birds about is marvellous; but in my experience, no single type of woman is attracted to racers. I've met old ladies who are just as turned on as young girls. I suppose women are always attracted by men who do physical things such as motor racing. It's a demonstration of control, speed, and danger and it has a glamour all of its own – which both sexes find exciting and stimulating. I personally have a respect for anybody who risks their lives. I think men share this respect – but for many women it turns to adulation.

Motor racing is an exciting spectator sport and truly international and this is one of the reasons why it is so successful. I think it's one of the most awe-inspiring sights to see all that latent power roaring up at the start of a Grand Prix – and then, in a split second, all the cars surging away.

I always have a bath on the night before a race. I do have them at other times as well, but I like to take things easy, have a quiet meal (usually at the same hotel I'm staying in) and then go to bed reasonably early at eleven or twelve o'clock. On the morning of the race I'm quite happy to rest in bed and read a book or the papers. I can't read French or most other languages so I'm a bit buggered there. There's no point in getting up too early when the circuit is nearby as there's nothing much to do. I might have an egg for breakfast and a glass of milk, and a very light lunch. I find it difficult to swallow solid stuff by lunchtime and so I might have some soup and then I'm ready to go to the circuit. You've already read what I'm like just before a race so we won't go into that again.

The strategy to employ during the race depends on how it's going. If you're not doing too well you may not be able to have any at all; but basically, it's a question of going as fast as you can. If you're chasing the leaders without making much impression, you just go flat out the whole time. You can achieve your top speed along the straights, of course, but when it comes to the corners you try to gain valuable seconds or fractions of seconds by making straights out of them. If we had to go round corners on fixed railway lines which followed the curves we'd lose a lot of time. We don't have to, thank goodness, so we're able to use all the road by starting the corner wide and then drifting the car through under accelerating power so that we clip the apex of the corner and continue the drift to the outside of the corner, nicely placed to enter the next straight. By using these tactics we've straightened out the corner and got through quicker. The technique

17. Prince Charles wanted to try his hand at driving a racing car.

18. Saving everything up for the race.

19. The Red Arrows are really close when you are up there with them!

TOP OPPOSITE   20. Tony Brise, a brilliant driver, was only half my age when I signed him up at twenty-three.

BOTTOM OPPOSITE   21. Samantha and Damon. There's nothing more relaxing than being with children.

ABOVE 22. Paul was over the moon about winning the race. He could easily have become a top racing driver.

23. I never won the British Grand Prix but came pretty close to it at Silverstone in 1960.

24. My back wheel fell off in my first Monaco Grand Prix in 1958. Since then I've won it five times.

25. 'You'll never win Indianapolis first time,' they said – but I did and I even talked them into putting doors on the loos.

26. Le Mans 1972 brought victory at my tenth attempt. Henri Pescarolo shared the driving, with Matra-Simcas taking first and second place.

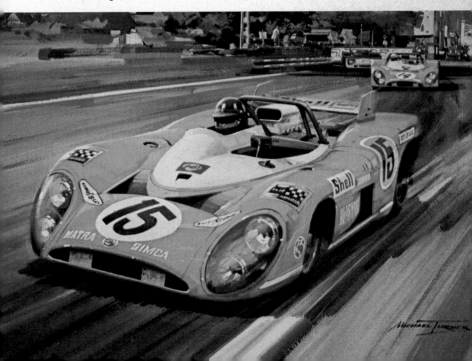

ABOVE LEFT   27. Never mind the weather. Bette timekeeping.
Dutch Grand Prix 1974.

ABOVE RIGHT   28. Damon had firm ideas on how helmets
should be fitted even at an early age.

BELOW   29. Damon, Samantha, Bette, Brigitte and her
godmother Fay Coakley.

of drifting calls for a very delicate balancing operation on the part of the driver in the use of the throttle to control the power through the rear wheels, and the steering wheel to control the front wheels to maintain the car in the required angle and direction, and get through the corner in the minimum of time.

If you're in the lead you want to know what's happening behind you, who is there and what you've got to contend with, and how the pattern of the race is sorting itself out. This is where your mirrors and pit signals come in, because your concentration is supposed to be on going as fast as you can.

I like to increase my lead to twenty seconds if I can and then I'm in a position to dictate the pace of the race. If you've got an even bigger lead, or you are a lap ahead perhaps, then you can ease off and settle down to a nice rhythm. You have more time to think. It seems like you've got all day when, in fact, you're only lapping a second a lap slower. It's amazing the difference a second makes on some tracks; it seems so slow – but it's the difference between driving ten-tenths and nine-tenths.

When someone starts pressing, you've really got to get yourself into peak again and this might take a few laps to get back to ten-tenths driving. It's certainly not boring, especially at those speeds. Nowadays, you can't let up or afford to give anything away. You've got to outwit and outdrive your competitiors on every straight and corner time and time again throughout the whole race.

It's a tremendous feeling if you win, but there are times when winning doesn't give much satisfaction. If the race has been handed to you on a plate, through the main opposition dropping out or breaking down through mechanical failures, you feel a bit of an impostor in receiving the acclaim. But there it is in the record books and that's not bad, I suppose. However, I'm not satisfied personally unless I know I've driven well, that the car's gone well, and I've beaten the opposition fairly in a race that wasn't too easy to win. It doesn't happen too often.

Would you be interested to know that I have another

bath after the race? It's one of the pleasures of motor racing: a good bath and then a nice meal. I like corn on the cob, mushrooms on toast, or bisque d'homard for starters and a thick juicy steak to follow. After the meal there's usually a high-spirited piss-up and that's always good fun. Jackie Stewart once said in an interview that there was a stage in my career when I constantly took my trousers down at parties. He must have a long memory because, way back in the sixties (when we were both driving for BRM), after I walked across the dining table in my underpants, I slipped on a wine glass and ended up with the shattered stem stuck well and truly in my leg with blood spurting all over the place. I don't think I've taken my trousers down at parties since.

During the Le Mans year of 1972 I was asked to speak in the City of London on 'Courage', of all things. Speakers on other occasions had included Group Captain Cheshire, vc, and Chay Blyth. I felt bloody uncomfortable. Courage is relative and I don't consider I'm any more qualified to speak on the subject than a woman who has given birth. Or a child, for that matter, who had to overcome its fear of the dark. I suppose they chose me to speak about courage because I'm a popular conception of it.

If my 1972 diary looked full, '73 was going to be even more crowded. Instead of twelve Grands Prix there were to be fifteen. Emerson Fittipaldi had ended the previous season as World Champion so it was only right that a Brazilian Grand Prix should be added in the following year. The other additions were a Swedish Grand Prix, and the Dutch one coming back in again.

13
An Embassy to Work from

They say lightning never strikes in the same place twice. During the last Grand Prix of the 1973 season I was bowling along at 150 m.p.h. during practice at Watkins Glen when the joint holding one of the back wheels snapped. It was impossible to control the car and I went careering off into the safety barrier . . . almost at the exact spot where I had broken my legs in the 1969 accident. This time, I stepped out unscathed but I wouldn't have done if they hadn't put a safety barrier there since my last prang.

The mechanics got the car repaired in time for the following day, but there was to be no joy in the race. François Cevert had been killed instantly in a terrible accident during practice. All of us had lost yet another good friend and none more so than Jackie Stewart, his team-mate and closest friend. François was only twenty-nine and one of the greats in motor racing. He had given up a talented career as a concert pianist and he was France's best racing driver. Only two years earlier he had won this United States Grand Prix. This time he was lying third in the World Championship and hoping to finish runner-up.

It was also to have been Jackie Stewart's 100th Grand Prix – but he and Chris Amon withdrew the team's Tyrrell-Fords from the race. Jackie Stewart had already collected enough points during the season to win the World Championship title for the third time; and he retired from the sport seven days later.

So far as the race was concerned, Ronnie Peterson won in a Lotus, with James Hunt second in the Hesketh March-Ford. Peterson started from pole position and Hunt put in the fastest lap. I only managed thirteenth place amongst the twenty-five starters.

When Jackie Stewart retired it made me feel bloody selfish. I think he was one of the finest racing drivers ever, if not *the* finest. He was out of a similar mould to Jimmy Clark and Stirling Moss. In addition to taking the World Championship Title three times, he won twenty-seven Grand Prix races and that was more than anyone else had done. I felt selfish because maybe I should have retired, too, for the sake of my family; but I was still enjoying being a racing driver. It was still giving me a tremendous amount of pleasure and satisfaction. It was a job I liked and got well paid for doing. It couldn't be said I was staying on just for the glory because I wasn't exactly setting the track alight with results.

Some drivers had retired in their thirties. Fangio went on till he was forty-seven. I was forty-four but as I was running my own racing team now with myself as driver and manager it meant that I was taking on a bigger responsibility than at any time before. It also meant even less time with my family, but neither Bette nor the children ever tried to stop me racing through anxiety or any other reason.

Bette was only nervous when she stayed at home. When she came to a race meeting she got tremendously involved with the time-keeping and what was going on – unlike Jackie Stewart's wife, Helen, who disliked racing. It must have been hell for her. There were times, of course, when Bette worried terribly when we went through bad patches and our close friends were killed. I'm sure she must have wanted me to quit – but if the thought crossed her mind it was dismissed because she never once suggested I should give it up. She understood I couldn't, any more than anyone can stop breathing. She knew it was something I had to do.

She was able to attend only some of the Grands Prix,

because she had the children to look after at home. Not being at the circuit made it harder for her, but it worked the other way for my mother. She came to one of my early races and as she was sitting in the stand someone turned to her and said: 'He's spun off.' When she asked: 'Who?' and they said 'Graham Hill' – that was enough. She left the stand and didn't want to see any more. My father came once or twice but he usually stuck it out on television at home throughout my career. By the end of a race he was a limp rag. The thing that really upset him was when the commentator said I was going to win a race, when there were still five laps to go. Although he'd never driven a car in his life he knew that anything could happen and that it frequently *did*. When I did well, both my parents were thrilled. They didn't like me racing but they never said anything or tried to stop me. When I won I could see they were proud.

It's difficult to assess what effect, if any, it had on the children. I don't think they felt any strain as they were born into and grew up with racing. Brigitte came to Silverstone when she was only seventeen days old. When she went on a horse-riding holiday some years later she told them that her daddy was Graham Hill. One of her friends pulled her up smartly and said: 'You shouldn't say that, it's bragging.' When she told Bette about it she said: 'I like to say who my daddy is. I'm proud of him.'

Our youngest child, Samantha, went through a phase of telling her school mates: 'My daddy's Graham Hill. Don't you know my daddy – he's Graham Hill the racing driver.' As the other children had famous sportsmen and television personalities as their fathers it was like water off a duck's back. Now that Samantha is older she'd be perfectly happy if she never went to another motor race. She doesn't want to *see* another racing car. Brigitte will come if Bette wants her to; so would Damon.

It must be difficult for them. It was tough on Damon, for instance, when he went to summer camps. The boys would point him out and say: 'That's Graham Hill's son,' but Damon wanted to be known as Damon Hill – not as

Graham Hill's son. He was proud of me, I'm glad to say, but he didn't want this acclaim.

I wish I could have spent more time with the children but even when I managed to have a day at home they were usually at school, and at week-ends or during the holidays I was busy racing. I didn't just tolerate my children, I don't mind admitting I adored them. I loved them for themselves and loved being with them. The short times I was able to be with them were the more precious and made me appreciate how lucky I was to have three healthy children. My life off the track, particularly that connected with charities, had brought me into contact with so many less fortunate spastic children, or children who had become disabled and I could never forget this.

I think that my career must have been tougher for Damon to take really. Being brought up in a home full of women meant that if he had any problem like a model aeroplane that wouldn't fly on remote control or something, no one around him had a clue how to put it right. So he was always asking when I would be home, or whether I'd be back that night. I wasn't around to kick a football about or play rugger with him. There were many times when I had to give my family second best – but they never grumbled and this made me appreciate them all the more.

Bette always wished I could have been home more often so that she could return some of the hospitality we received from others. We did have parties every now and again. usually big ones, but she would have liked to have put on more small, intimate dinner parties. We had a lovely home and although she wished we could use it more to entertain she knew, like me, that you can't have everything in life. I was even away practising for the German Grand Prix on the day that Bette and the family moved into our new home.

When I do manage to be with my family we always seem to be surrounded by people. That's no bad thing because Bette and I both enjoy crowds. But I know she wanted me to go away on holiday with her and the chil-

dren more. I've taken them to Italy when I've gone there
for the Grand Prix at Monza, as they were still on their
school holidays then. I find I'm an absolute washout for
the first two or three days on the rare occasions when I do
manage to go away with the family. I just go woomph –
I'm like a zombie. I don't want to do anything; I'm use-
less. I switch off from all thoughts of racing and just sort
of loaf about and don't want to do anything. Then, of
course, I pick up and I'm fine. Sometimes I managed a
one-day holiday and would fly to wherever the family
happened to be.

The whole business of setting up my own Shadow team
and finding the mechanics and a workshop, and arranging
transportation, took up a lot of time and effort at the
beginning of the 1974 season. I was also fully occupied
trying to find a sponsor. To start with I was naïve enough
to think I could do it without a sponsor, but there was no
way; it would take a fortune. So I approached a number
of people and firms and spoke to and lunched with lots of
boards of directors and that's how, eventually, I came to
be with Embassy. As I had been approached to become
the ambassador of motor sport to help promote it inter-
nationally, it seemed obvious that I ought to have an
embassy to work from.

Finding a sponsor is the first problem. Once you've got
one, the next thing is to control the money and make sure
it's spent in the best possible way. I found a workshop at
Woking and then it was a race against the clock to get
ready on time. Until December of the previous year it had
never occurred to me to think about running my own team.
I had always thought of myself as a racing driver, not an
entrant. Usually one tries to get all these things fixed long
before the start of the next season, allowing plenty of time
to build and test the cars.

It was soon obvious that we would have to miss the
first Grands Prix in January, February and March, so we
aimed to be ready for the Spanish Grand Prix at Barcelona
at the end of April. It would still be a push to make it, but
we managed to get it all together in three months.

Eventually we reached the splendid moment for painting the name GRAHAM HILL on the car; and I thought it would make the car look faster if this were in italics. The sponsors didn't, and we finished up with straight lettering. As we had two cars, with me as the sole team driver, and I intended to have two drivers with back-up cars for the following season, I had one tactical advantage. I let it be known around the circuits that I would be looking for a team mate and as I would be driving in the races I would be able to observe the talent from a fairly good seat. So it was possible some of the drivers might be a little more polite. Who knows, I might get better treatment.

Earlier, when I had been talking to prospective sponsors, I was approached by Tony Maylam, who was at that time a film director with Cygnet Films. He'd done quite a few motor racing films and he wanted to do an hour-long documentary profile on me – on and off the circuits, but not *all* my outside activities, I'm glad to say. He had a deal lined up with ATV, and the programme was scheduled to go out on the independent television network early the following year. It seemed a good way to promote motor racing itself and I agreed.

Then what happened? The film unit came out to Barcelona and I came nowhere. Here they were, supposed to be filming a success story, and there I was at the back of the grid, having to make numerous pit stops, at the lowest point in my career. They might just as well have run the end titles and settled for the closing music.

In fairness to the mechanics and everyone who had worked so hard on the car I should say that there just hadn't been time to do all the testing we'd hoped for, and the race itself was the first chance I'd really had to try the car, not having raced, myself, for six months. It needed a lot more development and I suppose the same could be said of me. I eventually went out with brake trouble.

My morale didn't exactly soar when the film crew went around the pits asking all the other drivers on camera what they thought of me. I learned afterwards they all thought I should have retired from racing while I was still at the top. I think one or two mentioned some good parties with me. One even went so far as to say he'd modelled his driving on mine – but I'm not too sure how he finished up in the placings.

Running one's own team was more difficult than I imagined and put a lot more pressure on me. Up to now I'd always been driving for somebody else. Now I had to bother about how the mechanics looked in the pits – if their overalls were respectable – and whether the car was nice and clean and would go. There was a tremendous responsibility, now I had sponsors. The fact that I had to get the team and car ready in such a short time added to the work load and made it a busy time. I can't pretend I didn't enjoy the new experience; it was most interesting and stimulating.

One of the drivers interviewed by the film-makers said I needed a challenge, something harder all the time, and that this was the force that made me tick. You'd be surprised at the number of psychiatrists in this business – but maybe there was some sense in what he said. He added that I was an idiot to become an entrant. I probably did need my bumps felt, because he'd been an entrant for some years and I'd seen him being ground down from time to time; so perhaps I should have learned from his experience.

The fact that the car was new was the chief problem. It wasn't a car that had been tried and found true around the circuits for some time. A lot of experimenting and adjusting still needed to be done to get it running and set up properly.

One of the most exciting things that happened in 1973 was the entry of Hesketh Racing on to the scene. Lord Hesketh is a big chap and he not only gave his bulk to the sport but also his money and a lot of it at that. He's a very jolly fellow and it was like a fresh breeze blowing through the scene. It's good to have characters like him around and I was delighted. I liked Alexander and his driver, James Hunt, very much and wanted to see them do well. When I first got into racing it wasn't nearly as professional as it is today. It had its colourful characters like Mike Hawthorn and Peter Collins, who were not only terrific drivers but always larking about together on and off the track. Hesketh Racing reintroduced this atmosphere and showed it was still possible to have fun and yet figure competitively in modern racing.

James Hunt started his Grand Prix career at Monaco that season and it was also a special occasion for me – my 150th Grand Prix; and that's where Tony Maylam and the film crew joined me.

The Monaco Grand Prix is the Ascot, the Derby, Cheltenham Gold Cup and Grand National of motor racing all rolled into one. It seems to grow and get even more exotic every year. I stay at the Hotel de Paris and I have the same room each year. It's like a second home and everyone is genuinely pleased to see you. I've raced at Monte Carlo so often I'm almost part of the furniture and the invitations flood in. The hospitality makes it very hard to concentrate on the racing.

A few changes in the circuit had been made for this year's race. They'd done a great job improving the pits. It was the first time I'd ever felt safe in the pit, with room to work. An extra Grandstand to seat another 9000 spectators had been added, but the altered circuit layout made it even more difficult to overtake. The race has always called for concentration and mental stamina and this year the tight, twisty circuit was likely to be even more demanding on both drivers and cars. Unless you're in the lead, the important thing during the first lap is to keep out of trouble. If you charge off, flat out, on the narrow course you're almost certain to end in a concertina. There were quite a few shunts in this one and although I was trying to keep out of trouble, with my one pair of eyes doing the work of six, someone got baulked in front of me and I had to stop.

This held me up, putting the pack even further ahead and I had to start chasing them hard. It took a while to get past some of them and then my brakes failed as I arrived at the chicane and I had to nip up the escape road. Back in the hunt, it meant braking early, which was a bit of a handicap. Then the car began to feel odd and I had to go into the pits. It was a puncture but even when the wheel was changed – the car still felt odd. I suspected another puncture and when I went into the pits, that's just what it was. Back in the race the car still felt bloody awful – and got worse and worse. I went into the pits again, but set off once more when the mechanics couldn't find anything wrong.

By now the car had got bloody dangerous and felt as though the rear wheels were steering. I had just decided to return to the pits when, of its own accord, the car suddenly turned sharp right, heading for the flag marshal who had to leap for his life. The mechanics found that a damaged suspension had in fact been steering the car. I'd covered sixty-two of the seventy-eight laps but had to retire, and that was the end of my 150th Grand Prix. And the film crew covered the whole non-event.

Jackie Stewart took the chequered flag and Emerson Fittipaldi was second. James Hunt, in his first Grand Prix, went well and looked like collecting some Championship points until his engine blew up when he was lying sixth, with only five laps to go.

After the race I followed my usual Monte Carlo pattern and went along to the prize-giving ceremony in the Hotel de Paris – then on for a couple of jars in the Tip-Top Bar, and to bed about four.

I always call in for a quick beer at Rosie's Bar before leaving the next morning. This is a very popular haunt of drivers and all the press and commentators, but that year, Tony Maylam wanted to include a scene in the film of me chatting with Prince Rainier and Princess Grace on the lawn of the Palais de Monaco. In past years it was often a case of them saying: 'Not again!' when they received me on the victory dais, but this year there wasn't much to talk about so far as the race and I were concerned. I think they probably saw a lot more of it than I did.

In one of the outside activities scenes in the film I had to go to a public house in Tottenham, the Olive Branch, to receive a £500 cheque for a Guide Dog for the Blind. I'm always ready to accept cheques, particularly when they're made out in my name – 'Graham Hill's Hard Luck Fund'. They had done a fantastic job in raising this sum. Some of them went on a sponsored walk and, if you saw the film, they were the ones on crutches.

If you watch a blind person finding his way with a white stick and another with a trained alsatian or labrador retriever, you can't help but notice the difference, not only in their mobility, but in their whole confidence. I take my hat off to everyone who raises money like this, either by selling raffle tickets, bunging money in the box, or going on sponsored walks. I only expected to stay at the pub for a few minutes but I was still there a couple of hours later in the middle of a sing-song.

Writers and film directors certainly delve deeply in order to get the human side of their subjects across on the screen. They took some film of me in the swimming pool at home and then asked me if I believed in God and dubbed my spoken thoughts over the scene.

I don't know about God – I really don't. I'm sure there must be a God. I can't prove there isn't and, similarly, I can't prove there is. I think religion serves a very, very good purpose in life; and I think it serves a greater purpose for some people than for others.

I said, at that moment, I didn't feel I needed religion. But if I was stuck in a boat in the middle of the Atlantic all by myself and had been there for days and was hungry and tired and cold without much chance of surviving, I know jolly well I'd start praying. So I know there is a God there for me. But I wouldn't say I was a practising Christian – though I'm certainly a Christian; so I suppose you could say I believe there is a God.

Television films with chaps walking on the moon set me thinking about the universe and the vastness of it and what a little speck we are here. And when I go into the garden and see all the flowers and hear the birds – I think there must be a God.

Later, they asked me if I believed in an after-life. I've

always thought that if there is one, then it's a bit of a bonus, something I hadn't quite expected. If there is – then, cheers – I'm all for it. I've enjoyed this one so much – I wouldn't mind having another. I'll find out eventually – but if there isn't I won't be disappointed because I shan't know too much about it, and it's not going to worry me; but, if there is one, that's good. I'll be delighted to hear about it. I'm looking forward to it – eventually.

When the film was put together and edited, after filming in Spain, Monte Carlo, England and the United States, I asked Tony Maylam who should narrate the film. He thought, for a world market, it would be better to go for a big American name. When I asked who he had in mind he said Paul Newman – so I picked up the phone in my study, then and there, and dialled Paul Newman at his home in Westport, Connecticut. He said: 'Fine,' and we were in business.

I had taken Paul Newman around Brands Hatch some time before and he told me that if he hadn't become an actor and a film director he would have wanted to be a racing driver. He'd done some amateur racing and when Tony Maylam and I flew out to meet him he was entered for a race at Pocono in Pennsylvania that week-end. We arrived just before the first practice and I got off my coat to set his car up for him, tweaking the suspension and that sort of thing. Then, after the practice, he went out and won the race at the age of forty-eight. He could easily have become a top racing driver if he had been pushed in that direction, rather than towards the screen, early in life. He was over the moon about winning the race and we all set off to celebrate, and then spent a couple of days at his home and got down to the narration.

We became good friends and did quite a bit of racing together after that, including world record runs on the Bonneville salt flats in Utah with the Ferrari team. We corresponded every other month or so. He'd tell me about his films and racing, and I'd tell him about my cars, team and things.

The *Graham* film was completed just before Christmas

and I showed it at home to a few friends, before it went out over the ITV network the following February and then world-wide. It was received very well and I thought the film-makers had done an excellent job, particularly with some of the shots of the races, which were mind-blowing. But it's always difficult watching something about yourself. I cringe, and feel a twit!

14

It's Always Someone Else

'HOW MUCH LONGER ARE YOU GOING TO BE 43. YOU'RE
WORSE THAN A WOMAN. YOU HAVE BEEN 43 EVER SINCE I
HAVE HAD THE MISFORTUNE OF KNOWING YOU. ADMIT YOUR
AGE. BEST WISHES ON YOUR 49TH BIRTHDAY.' That shows
the sort of friends I have. There were a lot of birthday
telegrams like that in 1974. The occasion, in February,
provided an excuse for two celebrations. A lunch in the
City with my father, then seventy-two, who was retiring
from the Stock Exchange after fifty-six years; and a party
at home for my *forty-fifth* birthday. Bette, Brigitte, Damon
and Samantha gave me a cake which was a real work of
art with a model of my car on it surrounded by four
miniature helmets, one at each corner, in my racing
colours. There were a lot of racing drivers and motoring
commentator friends as well as one or two other sportsmen – and that other British institution, Eric Morecambe
and Ernie Wise. They only have to stand there to make
you laugh. They were busy on their book and I took the
trouble to read it when it was published. It wasn't too
much trouble because they both gave me a copy of it, at
separate times – but within an hour of each other. David
Niven gave Bette and me a copy of his book, too, after
we'd stayed with him in Switzerland.

I moved my racing team from the Woking workshop,
which we had been sharing, to one of our own at Feltham
and switched from Shadow to Lola cars for the 1974
season, still under Embassy Racing sponsorship. I drove

in all fifteen of the Grands Prix and finished in eleven of them, but collected only one World Championship point for coming sixth in the Swedish Grand Prix.

In racing, you have to be honest with yourself. You're the only one who knows what sort of performance you're giving and you must decide whether it's the car or yourself that is failing to get up front. It's not always easy to do this, the dividing line can be very fine, but you've got to analyse it and be fair to both yourself and the car and then consider how you can improve things.

They must have thought more of me in the City than they did on the race tracks – because I was given the Freedom of the City of London in October. It's one of the things you can still get for free nowadays. Obviously, it's something I was very proud of. Having been born in Hampstead I consider myself a Londoner, and to be made a freeman was a great honour.

By now I was getting over six hundred invitations a year to attend functions, open fêtes and new garages, and make speeches. These, together with the Grands Prix, meant travelling about 150000 miles a year. So I started helicopter lessons. It would save a lot of time to take off from my home and land exactly where the engagement was.

When I was asked by Larry Webb to be a helicopter pilot in the Alistair MacLean film *Caravan to Vaccares* the manoeuvres I was directed to carry out made me look a bit of an ace at the game. It's amazing what illusions can be created on film. I enjoyed my helicopter lessons but I had to give them up as there were more pressing things to do.

I did manage to take an hour off one day, though, to have a go in a Tiger Moth which belonged to a friend at Elstree. Having flown one I can understand why the RAF pilots who learnt to fly on them still rave about them. With the open cockpit this was real flying. It felt as though I was in the cockpit of my racing car – but with wings.

I could have used a pair of wings when I went in for a

race that was part of a three-day rally shortly afterwards. I was sitting in my car on the grid, waiting for the starter to drop his flag, when some bloke behind thumped me. He'd jumped the start and I hadn't even moved!

There was another series of films for television with Tony Maylam and Cygnet Films in 1974. They were six half-hour programmes for ATV on advanced driving. I was glad to be asked to do this as it's a subject close to my heart. Ninety per cent of all road accidents are caused by human error and incorrect driving. So it follows that one of the best ways of reducing accidents is for us all to drive better – and behave better when driving. When I say that I include myself, naturally.

No one becomes a good driver by chance. It takes practice and this is where advanced driving comes in. It covers the real art of driving. I took the Institute of Advanced Motorists' Test – and became a member of their Council (so you can guess I passed)! I think it's a very good thing when motorists take the trouble to go on better driving and advanced driving courses and take voluntary tests like these. Anything that helps increase the standard of driving and safety on the roads and reduce the appalling accident statistics must be good. Motorists should be encouraged rather than beaten over the head all the time.

When we read of dozens of vehicles being involved in a series of multiple pile-ups in fog on a motorway we're all horrified at the casualties; but, in my opinion, to refer to it as 'motorway madness' is completely negative. No one considers themselves mad. When people go around talking about motorway madness they are obviously talking about someone else. It's *always* someone else, never themselves. So if everyone thinks that, then no one is to blame. It only encourages people to go and do the same thing – driving too fast and too close together – and this is criminal!

We covered most things in the series, including driving in difficult conditions such as on wet and slippery roads, on snow and ice, and in fog and mist. But when you are engaged for one particular morning to demonstrate driving in the snow in Hertfordshire, how do you make sure it's going to be snowing? You go to bed – and wake up the next morning to find snow, just as we did! It was about the only day it snowed in that area the whole winter, but there it was – on the dot. By mid-day, when we had finished filming, it had all gone. Fog, when booked ahead for a precise date, might seem difficult to arrange, too; but that was easy. The film crew produced a fog-machine and I must say I found driving through the gloom they created very realistic.

It's terrible to think of the numbers of children killed or injured on the roads. It seems ridiculous that we spend vast sums of money educating them and do not teach them adequately to be on guard on the roads. For one of the programmes, we filmed at a fabulous off-the-highway Road Safety Driving Centre built on the site of a former refuse tip by the London Borough of Harrow. All sorts of courses are run there and one of them is provided free to every school in the area, with a series of talks and practical lessons (in school time) for sixteen-year old pupils. Some of the periods are spent in driving simulators, before going on to the real thing. Then three at a time go in the cars with the instructor to become familiar with the car and most road conditions. These include roundabouts, cross-roads, hills, one-way streets, traffic lights, all on the site – *off* the public highway. The two pupils in the back can learn a lot from the instructor's advice before they take their turn at the wheel. They often absorb more because, unlike the driver, they don't have the strain of operating the controls while concentrating on the road situation.

If young learners are taught how to drive safely, with plenty of practice – instead of just learning how to pass the test – they are more likely to become – and stay – good drivers. The idea here is to bring the learner to a point where he or she can get full value from a regular driving school.

I would like to think that other councils and authorities could do something similar if they have an old refuse tip or a bit of waste land to spare. I feel very strongly that motoring should be included in a school's curriculum; first, because it's exciting for the children, and second because it protects our investment in a great asset – the young people of the nation.

The emphasis at this Centre isn't only on young drivers. There are courses for adult learners, as well as better driving, advanced driving and night driving courses for those who want to develop their skills further.

I'm sure that if drivers practise to improve their driving they'll not only enjoy it more – but other road users will also appreciate it – and the roads will be safer for everyone.

I enjoyed doing these television films and when completed they went out as a series over the ITV network. A book *Advanced Driving with Graham Hill* was published the following year, in 1975, aimed at helping *everyone* whether they had been driving for a few months or many years, and I hope it's helping a lot of people to complete their journeys in safety.

I had a unique experience at the Transport and Road Research Laboratory in Berkshire one day in 1974: I went bowling along in a car without a driver. It's not as crazy as it sounds. The car was guided at speeds of up to 80 m.p.h. by an energized cable buried beneath the road surface which controlled the steering and speed, as well as the spacing between one vehicle and another. It was one of several vehicle automation systems being developed and tested by the TRRL with other organizations and industry.

Automatic control systems are likely to result in more reliability and fewer accidents. They offer more accurate steering which would allow more traffic lanes on existing roads with stress-free, high-speed travel. The vehicles would be driven in the normal way on minor roads – and switch to the automatic mode on major roads and motorways. Automatic control of road vehicles, in fact, could take many forms. Although likely to be introduced in gradual stages, it could be in widespread use by the end of the century.

The year 2000 is a long way off, though, and in the

meantime road safety will still depend on our personal skills. I seem to have pushed this safe driving business a bit; but it *is* important. It affects every one of us, whether we're drivers or pedestrians.

Something that wasn't improving much was my golf. My handicap was still twenty-four; but I had little time to play while running my own racing team. I did come third in the American Golf Tournament of Grand Prix Drivers and Constructors once and, with a handicap like mine, one might well wonder how. It must have been one of my rare better days.

I love playing golf – and I enjoy fishing though I wouldn't call myself a real fisherman. I do a bit of fishing near my home, and took a day off towards the end of the Grand Prix season to go trout fishing, which I found very relaxing. I've done some salmon fishing on the West coast of Ireland and in Scotland, but I've never caught one.

In the winter I enjoy taking part in shoots, and I like to bag a pheasant. Still more, I like walking about the fields. That's natural, I suppose, since I've spent most of my life walking about pavements and race tracks. It's a competitive sport which requires skill and it makes for a very pleasant day out. Bette gets a bit fed up sometimes when I leave pheasants and muddy boots on the floor and disappear leaving someone else to clear up the mess.

Although I love being out in the countryside, I don't really know anything about farming; this can be a handicap, as I often get invited to speak at NFU dinners. On such occasions I usually find it best to let the farmers start by firing questions at me. Then I can talk about what they want to hear rather than bang on about something that might not interest them. I'm always ready to answer any questions – except on money!

At one NFU dinner someone brought up the subject of shooting and I told about the time I bought my first gun. I blasted away at everything but failed to hit anything. The next day I took the BRM on the track for practice and bagged a pheasant in the first lap.

I suppose my real hobby is my business – but around that time people were asking me, with regular monotony, when was I going to retire? The only time I thought about retirement was when people came up and asked me about it. I was still enjoying motor racing and the idea of giving it up never occurred to me. So all my thoughts and energies were concentrated towards continuing to be a racing driver.

Another question that annoyed me was when people asked how I justified motor racing. I don't have to. One might just as well ask why people race yachts, or horses, or each other? People like to do different things and I see no reason why they shouldn't, so long as the activities they follow aren't harmful or corrupting.

I continued motor racing because I enjoyed it physically and mentally. I enjoyed the stimulus, the physical sensation, the controlling of a racing car at high speed and the whole business of trying to do it better than someone else.

Society tells us to behave in a certain fashion and we all wear a thin veneer of civilization; but underneath we have instincts that have been there for years, and the ability to overcome danger is one of them that we need to satisfy. If we periodically experience physical danger in our hobbies, jobs, and other walks of life and find ourselves able to cope with and overcome our fears, I think we are all better for it. That's why I think it sensible to encourage young people to go out and do something adventurous. They become better balanced and less frustrated and are less likely to take part in demonstrations or join riots. They learn to appreciate life more and get more out of it.

If someone attempts to climb a rock face without learning how to do it first and taking all the necessary safety precautions – I wouldn't call that adventurous; it would be plain bloody stupid. They would also be putting other people's lives at risk in rescuing them. Going for a walk across the moors may seem a harmless enough pastime but unless the walkers know what they're doing, where they are, and where they're going – it can be equally dangerous. The newspapers are full of stories of people getting lost and suffering from exposure through having to spend a night out in fog, mist, or a blizzard – very often when they're only a few hundred yards from shelter or civilization. There's no point in anyone sticking their neck on the line foolishly. There's only point to it when they know the risks and take all possible precautions. If they meet danger under those circumstances they will be well prepared to cope with it and they will get satisfaction from having coped – both with their fears and the problems.

Motor racing provided me with that outlet and it's a sport that's growing and attracting more interest all the time. It's a sport *and* an industry; and countries all over the world are queuing up to stage Grand Prix races. In America, motor racing is second only to horse racing as the most popular spectator sport.

The sport has benefited enormously from the sponsors coming in. Originally, we had trade sponsors but in more recent years we've had more and more outside sponsors coming in who appreciate the benefits to themselves and their products. This fresh injection of money has helped to transform the sport in colour, in prize money, in facilities and in spectator interest. More circuits are being built and we're being asked to compete in more events. The whole business of sponsorship is a highly specialized subject and the benefits are not always obvious. It struck me as a bit odd, for instance, to see a Brazilian bank advertising themselves on Emerson and Wilson Fittipaldi's cars at all the Grands Prix. Odd, that is, until I learnt that Brazil were booking satellite time to transmit film of each Grand Prix back to South America.

Sponsors are doing motor racing an enormous amount of good; but it's up to the drivers and teams to satisfy them in return, not only in the races but also off the tracks as well. When Wills Embassy sponsored me I soon realized I would need to be something of a businessman. This was new to me as, until then, I had been a works driver and the only person I had to deal with then was the team manager.

Once sponsored, new horizons opened up and I found myself having to talk to a whole lot of new people – businessmen. I found it very stimulating and exciting. I didn't know I had any ability as a businessman up to that point. Then it seemed to slot itself into place.

Besides the main sponsor, there are usually trade sponsors who support you by supplying various items of equipment for the car such as fuel, oil, brakes, shock-absorbers, sparking plugs, and tyres and they want smaller advertising space on the car. You can say you don't want any more stickers on your car, of course, but then you will be faced with having to buy all their products.

The main thing about motor racing is that it is a spectacle. It has high entertainment value. More and more people are coming to watch and the club memberships of people who want to take part in various forms of racing is mounting each year. The very fact that we're required to race almost every week-end throughout the world, and often on week-days, means that the organizers are getting enough people to come and see the races. With this, in turn, enabling them to afford to fly the drivers and cars over – with bigger and bigger prize money.

There's also an indirect benefit. Motor racing has a happy knack of getting things done ten times quicker than they would be done normally. Racing drivers want results today – not tomorrow. So they're continually beating the tyre technicians over the head to get better tyres, and the engine designers for more efficient combustion and power, the metallurgists for better metals, and the oil men for better fuels. As a result of all this we have tyres on our ordinary cars with better wet-weather grip, better suspensions, shock absorbers, brakes, fuel and fuel-injection systems, engines and oils. We would have had them anyway, but motor racing has helped to get them that much sooner.

But I wouldn't attempt to put motor racing forward, mainly, as a means of progress. That comes second; for without the paying customers there wouldn't be any motor racing. So we have to satisfy the spectators first, and then let the progress come along with it.

Any country that does well in motor racing has a wonderful shop window – and the wise ones hang their hat on it.

30. Phew – you have to be fit to stroke a boat-race crew. I joined Oxford over the course in 1975.

31. I would have loved to have been around in the pioneering days when man first learnt to fly.

TOP OPPOSITE 32. I swim to keep fit – but if I was lost at sea, without much chance of surviving, I know jolly well I'd start praying.

BOTTOM OPPOSITE 33. I fancied myself a bit. A *pas de deux* with Carol Hill (no relation) – a principal dancer with the London Festival Ballet.

RIGHT 34. A gesture, older than some people think, to the American commentator who referred to me as a veteran.

BELOW 35. Anything happens with Eric (Sykes). Sean Connery, Ronnie Carroll, Stanley Baker – guests at a Tunis Golf Club.

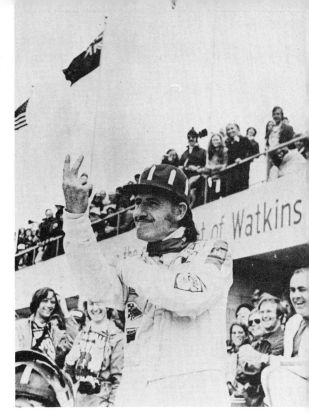

36. Gun-dog Sandringham Bel, with her master.

37. I hate throwing anything away. Stuff collects in my study and all over the place.

15

Retirement

Running a two-car team was my main preoccupation during 1975 and I recommend it to anyone as a sure-fire way of getting ulcers. Our finishing record during the previous year was better than any of the other teams, with nineteen finishes from twenty-seven starts, but those are just statistics which make their way into the record books. They didn't win races.

Rolf Stommelen, my team-mate in the Embassy Lola team, had driven in the last four Grands Prix the previous year and gone very well. He also did well in the South African Grand Prix and the Race of Champions at the start of the 1975 season. But as so much of the design work on the Lolas had been done by Andrew Smallman – we decided to establish ourselves as constructors in our own right. We re-named the car the Embassy-Hill GH1 and a second one was completed just in time for the International Trophy at Silverstone. Andy and the mechanics did a first-class job and we had a trouble-free run first time out.

I drove in the Argentine Grand Prix in January (this was my 175th Grand Prix), and in the Brazilian one a couple of weeks later. I should have raced in the South African one but the car went out of control during practice and was written off. I stood down as a driver for the Spanish Grand Prix to manage the team. The French driver François Migault drove the first GH1 model and Rolf Stommelen the GH2. The race was marred by an appalling tragedy when Rolf's car lost a rear aerofoil at 150 m.p.h., struck the top of the safety barrier, and flew off the track killing and injuring spectators. The accident was almost a carbon copy of those which Jochen Rindt and I had at the same spot in 1969, when we both lost our rear wings. Rolf, who had been leading the field until the race was stopped, was trapped in the smashed cockpit, upside down, but the car's fire extinguishing system prevented it from catching fire. Happily, he made an astonishing recovery from the severe leg and other injuries he sustained and was back, within four months, driving for me in the Austrian Grand Prix – which says a lot for his courage and determination.

In the interests of safety after the Barcelona incident, at the Monaco Grand Prix the field for the actual race was cut down to the eighteen fastest cars in practice. It was my eighteenth appearance there but I failed to qualify. This was naturally a big disappointment; but I enjoyed the practice.

I also enjoyed watching the brilliant performance of Tony Brise in the Formula 3 race there. This got him rave notices and all the teams were after him with contracts – but they were too late. I had already shaken hands the night before on a deal with him to join my team.

I had been very impressed with a drive of his at Silverstone earlier in the season and he'd also shown up well in his first ever Formula 1 drive in the Spanish Grand Prix before the race was stopped. Tony had started kart-racing when he was eight and was winning championships at twelve. He started motor racing at eighteen and by the time he had graduated with an honours degree in business administration from Aston University, Birmingham, he had swept the board in twenty-five Formula Ford races, with a total of over fifty wins in four years of motor racing in various Formulas. Whatever type of race he entered, Tony seemed unbeatable. His father had been world stock car champion three times, so it must run in the blood. He made his first Formula 1 trip with my team in the Belgian Grand Prix but dropped out with engine failure. In the Swedish Grand Prix he came sixth and claimed his first World Championship point.

Seeing him as a potential World Champion, I was delighted to sign him up on a two-year contract. He was only twenty-three which was half my age and yet here he was in Grand Prix racing at an age before I'd even driven a car. His flair, competitive spirit, car control and maturity of driving belied his comparative youth. I think him one of the most exciting drivers that Britain has seen for many years. Bette and I got on well with Tony and his wife Janet; we all clicked the moment we met – which was great.

Once you come out with a new racing car design you can spend years developing it. I had a young team and our prospects looked as though we could begin to be really competitive. Andy Smallman was twenty-four and a brilliant designer. He kept the design of the new car simple, went all out for reliability, and probed the smallest detail to get it right. Ray Brimble, my team manager, had a tremendous amount of experience in motor racing. He was an ideal right-hand man and ran the racing division. I was also fortunate in having a first-class team of mechanics and back-up people at our Feltham works and all were tremendously enthusiastic.

One of the hardest decisions any Grand Prix driver has to make is when to retire. I've always found that one of the best places to make decisions is in the bath, and that's where I made up my mind to retire. It was after the practice for the Belgian Grand Prix. I'd been tremendously impressed with Tony Brise's performance that day and as I was running my own team I felt I ought to be in the pits to back up my drivers and make sure that they and the new cars did well. If I continued to drive in the team I wouldn't be able to do this and, although I was still enjoying being a racing driver, I would really only be indulging myself.

The next problem was when to make the announcement. I was forty-six and I'd driven in over 700 races, which included 176 Grands Prix, which was more than any other driver; but Fangio hadn't retired until he was forty-seven. If I wasn't enjoying driving it would have been

easy, but I still had an idea in the back of my mind that
I might want to come back into Formula 1 racing once
I'd got the team going and established. The idea was only
a dream, though, and I realized it just wasn't on.

When I told Bette I was going to announce my retirement on the eve of the British Grand Prix at Silverstone,
she said: 'Oooh – mmmm – that's sad isn't it.' Her
reaction surprised many people who thought she would
have breathed a sigh of relief; but she had a very balanced
outlook on motor racing and never allowed herself to
think of me having an accident or getting hurt. She knew
it could happen, of course, because it frequently did, but
never allowed it to cloud her mind. We both enjoyed
motor racing and it had given us a wonderful life.

If making that decision was difficult – I found my slow
retirement lap round Silverstone, just before the British
Grand Prix, more so. I had my helmet off and by the time
I got to the first corner I had a lump in my throat because
of the terrific reception from the crowd. I was so choked
I couldn't see. When your face starts to contort it's not
easy to keep smiling. I told myself, 'Buck up, you bloody
twit, and smile.' I tried to but when you feel like crying it's
difficult – and I must have looked a bit bloody odd. Anyway, I managed to keep this terrible grin on my face
until I returned to the pits – but it was murder.

When I watched Tony go out to the grid for the Grand
Prix that was another bad moment – knowing I wouldn't
ever be out there again. But when I concentrated on how
well he was doing it occupied my mind and made it a lot
easier. He started in thirteenth place and overtook two
cars on the first lap. By the tenth he was lying eighth.
During the early laps his was the fastest car on the track –
but then it rained. Part of the track was still dry but, in a
deluge on the far side, Tony shot round a corner and found
himself aquaplaning and driving like a rudderless boat.
He zoomed off into the catch fencing at around 100 m.p.h.
and was knocked out by one of the wooden stakes which
ripped off his helmet.

Shortly afterwards there were multiple shunts all over

the place with most of the sixteen drivers who crashed doing so in the rain before the race was red-flagged to a premature end. Some plunged into the catch fencing at high speed – others aquaplaned out of control at a mere 10 m.p.h.

Tony had sustained a nasty crack on his head and we had to organize an air-ambulance to take him to Stoke Mandeville Hospital. Janet went with him and, happily, the medical check-up showed his injuries were limited to heavy bruising of the face and a cut above the left ear which needed seven stitches.

The multiple shunts caused so much confusion that there was a long-drawn-out dispute as to who finished where in the placings, but there was no doubt about the winner. Emerson Fittipaldi had led the last thirteen laps and he was still in the lead when the race was stopped after fifty-six laps.

I was so bloody happy with Tony Brise's performance during the ninety minutes of the race that I forgot all about my retirement. It confirmed everything I had believed – that he was likely to become a future World Champion.

It was disappointing not to have won the British Grand Prix during my own career as a driver; but that's the way the cookie crumbles. I came pretty close to it, finishing second twice and third twice. I would have liked to have won the Grand Prix in my own country, naturally, but failures make you appreciate the successes more. Having won fourteen Grands Prix and 289 World Championship points I hadn't any cause for complaint.

Looking back, the five races that stood out that I was really pleased about were: the German race in the rain; the Monaco Grand Prix which I won after having to get out and push the car back into the race; the Indianapolis victory; coming sixth in the South African Grand Prix after my accident and all the work on that bicycle – and winning Le Mans, which gave me the Triple Crown.

Running a racing team is very time-consuming, particularly when you've got a new team and new cars. While

Rolf Stommelen was recovering from his injuries, Alan Jones took his place. He had a lot of successes in various formulas and, later, gave my team our best result with a fifth place in the German Grand Prix. Tony Brise had to retire in that race but was well up among the leaders in the other Grands Prix. He still did some Formula 5000 racing – and won the John Player Formula Atlantic Championship in 1975 which gave even further proof of his skill and adaptability. He also got hooked on flying and wanted to learn.

Both of us went to Long Beach, California for a Formula 5000 race at the end of September. Tony was driving in it and I was given the title of Grand Marshal. The reason for this was that it was to be a street race around the Long Beach waterfront – rather similar to Monte Carlo. This had never been done before and as I had won Monaco five times they wanted me to act as an adviser to help them set up the new race.

They not only gave me that grand title, but a grand residence to go with it. I'd never been on the *Queen Mary* and it seemed ridiculous that I had to go to America to do so, but that's where they put me – in a little bit of old England sitting there in Long Beach. They use the liner as a hotel and museum and it's open to the public for tours and that sort of thing. The underwater scenes there were designed by Jacques Cousteau and the whole thing is most impressive. There are 400 cabins and they use it as a Conference Centre as well. They spent a fortune on the ship and did a lot of things wrong at first. When they took the engines and gear out of her the whole thing started to buckle and it completely upset the balance of the ship. They had to put in concrete to put things right but they ended up with an excellent job.

Many people feel we should have kept the *Queen Mary* in England and used it as a hotel and conference centre ourselves. It would be nice to have it but I think it's doing more good in the States. The Americans are better at these things than we are. They have the flair, enterprise, and initiative. They see the value in them, and have the money to match the bright idea. They don't just talk – they've bloody done it!

I felt proud to be in a British ship and enjoyed staying in her and acting as an adviser to the race. Long Beach is rather like Bournemouth; and they told me they wanted to give the place a social identity of its own. Some go-ahead people decided to get the council and local residents to go along with them and put on this street race. It meant closing the shops for a while and one or two people didn't like the idea of being put out of business; so what did the authorities do? They offered to ship anyone who didn't want to stay to Las Vegas for the week-end. They thought they would have a stampede – but only a few dozen elected to go. The whole place was proud to be in on the event and Long Beach got just what it wanted, a tremendous amount of publicity.

I was proud, too, to be associated with the race and their enterprise and did my best to give the sort of advice they needed on safety and so on and also did a lot of television, radio, and press interviews to help promote the race. I even did an interview with Barrie Gill for BBC Radio 2 while I was still in bed. I wasn't being lazy, it was just damned early.

The streets were wider than Monaco's and there was a long straight of just under a mile which meant the cars could do well over 170 m.p.h. along the sea front. Tony Brise did a fast practice, and during the early part of the 100-mile race he was in second position. It was a very demanding course with no room for error and the rain which came after the first lap made things a bit dodgy. When Tony moved up into the lead he was challenged by Andretti several times but managed to hold his position. It was a tremendously exciting race, watched by 60000 people who had seats, and by thousands more all around the circuit. It was quite fantastic to see the old retired people sitting along the pavements and being just as excited about the cars flashing by through their streets as the younger motor racing enthusiasts.

Tony spun at one of the turns and let Andretti through –

but regained the lead and held it until he went out later with mechanical trouble. For once I didn't have to worry about a car breaking down as this was nothing to do with my team, but I was sorry to see him go out, as he had put on a fabulous race and given the crowd their money's worth. If he couldn't win it was good to see another Englishman do so. Brian Redman won not only the race – but his second straight Formula 5000 series Championship.

I was even more delighted, about that time, when Wills Embassy agreed to continue their backing of my Formula 1 team for the 1976 Grand Prix season. It takes a few years to get a team going and now it was really beginning to happen. This would be my fourth year with Embassy and, this time, the team was going to be confined to a single car entry for Tony Brise. The first of the team's 1976 cars was almost ready at the Feltham works – and Tony was ready to start the development testing when he returned from Long Beach and the final Grand Prix of the '75 season in America at Watkins Glen that followed shortly afterwards. The plan was to construct three new cars and take two to all the Grands Prix, and use the third as a development car.

Tony tested the first in late October and, as I watched, I was delighted with the car's performance and the way Tony handled it. I would have liked to have had a go myself – but having decided to retire . . . that was that. I did miss the physical sensation of controlling a Formula 1 car, though, through the corners and down the straights and I missed the competitive stimulus. It was something I'd done all my adult life and to stop suddenly was quite a wrench.

We also had some luck with the other kind of racing in 1975. Horse racing is a lot of fun and although I don't consider myself a gambler I almost went through the card once – with five winners in six races at one meeting. I've had some quite big wins since; but, in my book, if you're going racing, do it in style if you can; and that's just what Bette and I did for the 1975 Derby. Ron Shaw picked us up off the lawn in a helicopter and flew us to

Epsom as guests of Lord Derby. I picked the Derby winner, which was an added bonus to a perfect day.

I used to go to the Cheltenham Gold Cup regularly with Charles Benson, 'The Scout' of the *Daily Express*. Whenever I get a hot tip it sends the old adrenalin surging; but when you are at a race meeting you've got to bet, haven't you? When Bette came with me she'd bet on each race. She'd tick off her favourites on the programme and hand it to me and if I asked, 'Where's the money, then?' she'd say: 'I'm not wasting the house-keeping on flipping horses,' and leave me to put a pound each way on the nags of her choice. I've been stuck with this lark ever since the first time it happened.

Our two daughters love horses. Brigitte had a horse which, though a boy, was given a girl's name on account of my racing car. To watch Lola and Brigitte jump was a real joy. They could have done well in show jumping, I think, but it's a highly competitive sport that requires total dedication and a lot of practice – like motor racing. Brigitte was busy with her O-level exams around this time and it's not fair to keep horses unless you're able to exercise them regularly; so she had to sell him. But Samantha still has old Blue Boy out in the paddock and boy – when he starts jumping well – he gets big-headed.

Damon got on her pony once and rode it like a cowboy but he's not really interested in riding, unless it's a motor-bike. He got his first motor-cycle at ten as a reward for passing the entrance exam to the school where he is a day boy, and since then he's become a bit of an ace at stunt riding. I took him to see Evel Knievel, the American motor-cycle stunt man, at Wembley stadium during the summer and it was terrific. That man really has guts – and skill – but on this occasion it didn't quite work out, and he fractured his spine after clearing thirteen London buses.

I used to do motor-cycle scrambles but now I'm more interested in trials, and so is Damon. He made quite a name for himself in the trials organized by Lord Hesketh after the British Grand Prix. Damon was fourteen, and the only school-boy competing against the experienced riders of Grand Prix racing mechanics and team managers. He tied for first place, with three others, but missed out in the tie-breaker. This was to be a dragster stop after the fastest speed over a short distance, and afterwards he said to the press: 'It was something I'd never done before and I shot over the line where I should have stopped, and skidded on the wet grass. If the tie-breaker had been "wheelies" – riding the bike with one wheel in the air – I think I might have stood a chance of winning; but as it was I came fourth.'

We practise together whenever we can, around the grounds and woodlands of our home. For me it's a way of relaxing and keeping fit. I've no intention of taking part in actual trials but in Damon's case it's for real. He hasn't had tuition from anyone and I think he's a natural. He has spent hours and hours watching the mechanics at work on my cars and he takes the whole motor-cycle engine apart and puts it together again to make sure everything is working properly before each trials meeting.

So long as he sticks to motor-cycle trials Bette will be happy and so will I. Neither of us wants him to become a motor racing driver. I can't believe that any parents want their son to go steaming into motor racing. I think Damon's too intelligent for that. He's got more brains than I have for a start. But it's his life and only fair to hear what he has to say about it: 'I don't know whether I want to ride motor-cycles for a living, and I don't know whether I am good enough. I've never tried racing driving so I don't know about that either. Cars are getting faster and faster and by the time I get old enough to drive I might have chickened out.'

Besides motor-cycling around our home, the grounds were used for a summer camp when we invited some of the lads from the Springfield Boys' Club over. One of the eight-year olds had never been on holiday before and he was so excited he kept everyone awake all night. They swam in the pool, and bounced on the trampoline, and I took them up for a flight in my plane at Elstree. They were great boys and we enjoyed their stay.

When I announced my retirement before the Silverstone Grand Prix I was very careful to mention Formula 1 driving. I didn't say anything about not driving any more in the odd saloon car race, or charity race. I fully intended to do some of that and I was looking forward to it. That would only be for fun, of course, because my number one priority was to get our Grand Prix cars going quicker and better than others.

16

Busier than Ever

No one knows what they can do until they try and, usually, the more you do – the more you find you can do. After I retired, I found myself working harder than at any time in my life and it made me wonder what the blazes I had done with the rest of my time; I must have been going through life at half-cock. As constructor, team director, and ambassador for the sport I really had to go steaming into it. I was still getting around 700 written invitations a year to attend functions, make speeches, give talks, and play in charity golf and cricket matches. A lot more invitations came over the telephone and on top of all this there were some 2000 letters a year to answer on every subject one can think of.

An evening at home was becoming a luxury and lots of other things had to go by the board. I used to lunch with friends once or twice a week at a club in London which was always a good jolly; but there was no more time for that any longer, nor was there time for much golf, which was a pity as I found an ideal partner in Larry Webb who lived nearby and became a good friend. His handicap was twenty-four and so was mine! I also had to turn down shooting dates which, for me, was unheard of.

The only way to fit in my working engagements was to stretch the day. When I got home late from dinners and functions I caught up on my reading and paper work and seldom went to bed before two a.m. I've never had any problem with sleep and I gather this is an asset. I thought

it was normal until I heard others discussing their difficulties getting to sleep. I can get by with five hours and
when I could I'd fix meetings for early morning. This
enabled me to drive into the centre of London ahead of
the rush-hour traffic – attend the meeting – and still have
time for a good morning's work on other engagements.

It's not always just a case of popping down the road,
though. After the American Grand Prix I had an invitation to go to a Murray Halberg Trust Dinner in New
Zealand. I suggested they should find someone closer to
home, perhaps, and save money for the charity – but
they said they had an arrangement with Air New Zealand
– so I went.

This was typical of the sort of life I was leading after my
retirement. I would be in New York on Sunday, Los
Angeles on Monday, then I crossed datelines and lost
Tuesday, and was in New Zealand for the dinner on
Wednesday. Then Sydney on Friday and Tehran on
Saturday. Iran might well be the first country in that part
of the world to own a professional racing circuit and I was
there helping to promote the idea.

A week later, back in England, I was on Michael
Parkinson's show. I wasn't happy with my performance
on it but several friends said they liked it. I hope they
weren't just being kind. I enjoy doing radio and television
shows, including panel games; but when you go on a chat
show or interview they often ask you to turn up for a dry
run first to go through the questions. When they do that,
I tell them I'm not coming. I react to audiences and the
bigger the audience the more I react. In my opinion a dry
run only dries you up. If you do it off the cuff, 'live' and
for real you'll be more natural and more likely to put on a
better performance.

I had a telephone call from the Deputy Director-
General of the Institute of Directors who asked if I would
speak at their annual convention at the Albert Hall, to an
audience which in the past had numbered 5000. There
was a pause – then perhaps he sensed he ought to add
something: 'Lord Erroll said you wouldn't turn down a

challenge.' Of course I didn't have the courage to say
'No,' and that was my first mistake. The second was when
he said, 'How much would you want, to come and speak?'
and I said rather grandly, 'I'll take the same fee as the
other speakers you've invited.' The reply was, 'Good –
they're coming for nothing.'

The last time I had performed in the Albert Hall was as
a boy scout in a gymnastic team. I was just the right bloke
for that occasion seeing that the sports I enjoyed most were
spent sitting down; and I felt equally qualified to speak on
this occasion, being a director myself . . . of various un-
profitable businesses!

When I stood up to speak I held out the official invitation card they had sent me and said: 'Gentlemen, I
hope you'll forgive me for bringing this up – and I don't
mean to embarrass anyone – but I do have some letters
after my name – but maybe you've left them out because
you thought they were for other bugger's efforts.' Then I
put down the invitation card (without the OBE on it) and
got on with my speech, mentioning that this was the third
time that morning I had got off a warm seat with paper
in my hand.

All the speeches made that day were published afterwards, word for word, in the *Director* magazine – mine too,
except for that bit. Maybe they thought it wouldn't look
good in print. Maybe you think so, too. Anyway, I
thoroughly enjoyed being there and felt honoured to be
speaking alongside so many eminent politicians and
captains of industry.

All these engagements had to be dove-tailed into the
work of running the team and testing the new car. Five
days later I drove to Elstree and flew myself and two
others to Silverstone to test and photograph the team's
new car. It was hopeless calling anyone 'Tony' at the
circuit as I got three answers – like Alpine echoes. Brise
was driving the car, Lord Snowdon was photographing it,
and Maylam turned up with a film crew. Tony Brise's
test drives gave us a lot of useful technical information on
the car, Tony Snowdon got some excellent colour photo-

graphs, and Tony Maylam was there to interview me on *A Fast Drive in the Country*. Since we last met he had formed his own company and that was the title of a film he was just completing on the heyday of Le Mans. James Coburn, the American actor, was hosting the film and doing some of the driving to reconstruct some of the scenes. With that sort of back-up and a chance to promote motor sport, I was delighted to be included.

Having flown Tony Snowdon and Tony Brise back with me to Elstree, I rushed home and had a quick bath and change and went out to an official dinner. I did some more paper work early next morning, before a newspaper interview at home. Then I flew to Cambridge for the opening of the new Patcentre laboratories by Prince Philip. This was a £1 million technology centre, set up by PA International, the management consultants, working with industrial clients on contract research. One of the companies, Sedgeminster Technical Developments of which I am a Director, was working with the centre on several energy-saving products, such as solar panels to heat water.

I became particularly interested in solar energy, reading and learning all I could about the subject. I think it's wicked the way precious natural fuel is being used, when we have that ball of fire up in the sky that no one is doing much with. I have strong views on this and, of course, expect to be criticized for them. Some question the fuel used in motor racing but I think that when people criticize anything they should do their homework and get the facts right first. What they don't seem to realize is that you can test and race twenty-five cars for a whole season for the Grands Prix and only use the same amount of fuel as a jumbo jet on a one-way trip from Tehran to London – and yet give pleasure to millions.

One of the other things produced by the company I was associated with was a battery-operated cycle that does twenty miles for a penny; and I demonstrated this to Prince Philip at the Centre. It was still in the prototype stage, but was capable of travelling at 20 m.p.h. It could go up a one-in-eight hill at 11 m.p.h. without pedalling, and recharge its battery when going down hill.

That afternoon I flew back to Elstree and drove to my office in London to deal with the mail before going out to a dinner in the evening. Next morning I set off for the Esso Sales Centre at Stoke Poges. Then on to a children's education television recording with Alvin Stardust. I was in my London office at 3 p.m. – then flew out of Heathrow at 6 p.m. for New York.

When I'm commuting between countries on jets I sometimes sleep, but not too much as I need to read a lot of things. Just then I was sitting on the government's Blennerhassett committee looking into the laws of drink and driving and, as we were just coming up to the draft of our final report, I had to read through all that.

The time difference on that flight meant I arrived in New York at the same time (by the clock) that I had taken off from London; and I was able to go straight into a meeting with the people I'd come to see at CBS. After a couple of hours I went back to the hotel for my five hours' quota of sleep, and continued the meeting with them at their offices early next morning. Then I spent an hour with forty sales executives to convince them of the pleasure, drama, and excitement of motor racing. After that I went to another meeting at CBS to sort out an agreement – which was the whole purpose of my trip – in which I was to act as a race interviewer for them in various countries at the Grands Prix during the coming 1976 season.

Having signed the contract we lunched together, after which I went off to meet another gentleman, an investment director in New York, to look at a car he wanted me to know about.

I caught the plane back home that Friday night and arrived at Heathrow at seven o'clock next morning. Got in the car and drove down for some game shooting in Kent. I spent that evening at home and on Sunday caught another jet for Vienna to open the Jochen Rindt Memorial Motor Show on Monday – and flew back home again that night.

Some people think I'm nuts to take on so much – and go steaming straight into it directly I get off a jet. But I think that if you go around talking about jet lag, you can talk yourself into being tired. I find that if I fly in from New York, say in the early morning, and sit down and people talk to me, I'm a bit slow with my answers, as I'm not thinking quite as sharply as I should be. But if, instead of just sitting around, I start working right away I can whizz straight through it and gain part of a day, or perhaps even a whole day. My mother is a ball of fire and I suppose that's where I get my energy from.

One of the television shows I went on after I retired was the BBC *Keepsakes* programme. They have a large trunk and you're invited to bring along things of interest that you've kept over the years. It was a bit difficult to know what to select as I'm a terrible hoarder. I can't throw anything away and I get into a lot of trouble for this at home. Some of the stuff collects itself in my study and the rest of it all over the place. I even keep old ties I know I'll never wear again.

In the end I picked out some photographs of the family, and a copy of one of my school reports – but, on reflection, the less said about that the better. There was a Royal Navy Certificate that showed I was capable of taking charge of a boiler-room, steaming at full power. We pulled the first World Championship cup that I won out of the trunk; the plaque from the Americans when they took me through the sound barrier; a colour photograph when I flew with the Red Arrows; and the newspaper plate when I won the Indianapolis 500; the bed sheet, too, with all the signatures on it that the hospital put up on the wall for me after my accident in 1969.

I also took the address book Bette gave me just before we were married with the inscription: 'For you darling, lest you forget – Bette – August 1954'.

They round off the show by asking you: 'If the house was on fire, and there was one keepsake you could choose to save, which would it be?' The photograph album – without question! I couldn't ever replace that. It has photographs dating back to when I was a boy, of Bette and our wedding and the children; so I'd save that album. There are so many memories in it.

Quite often, when I'd been away from home for some time, I'd meet someone who'd say, 'That was a super dinner party at your place the other night.' It made me feel a bit of an idiot because I didn't know anything about it. When I said to Bette, 'You didn't tell *me* you had a dinner party,' she would say, 'Oh . . . no. Well, I haven't seen you to tell you, have I?'

One evening she did tell me she had invited my golfing partner Larry Webb and his wife Margaret to dinner. They were going to be away for six weeks or so in Australia. I was a bit put out and said: 'What did you do that for?'

'They're off in a couple of days – it's the only night we could fix. If you've got a date – hard luck. It's not our fault if you can't make it.'

I wasn't expected back from my date in London until midnight or so, but it's amazing how you can hustle a meeting along when you have to – and I managed to get home and surprise them at the brandy stage. It turned into just the sort of evening I enjoy at home, with good company and plenty of chat, and before we knew what had happened it was three o'clock in the morning.

No one really likes to miss out on something. I don't, Bette doesn't – who the heck does? When a crowd of boys are after autographs there are always front runners who elbow the others out. Whenever I can, I try to reach one or two of the boys at the back who are either shy, or who haven't got the necessary push, who would otherwise miss out.

One group of people who continue to miss out are the disabled. This is one of the few things that really gets under my skin. I don't want to start arguments here, but I've campaigned along with a lot of other people for the Disabled Drivers' Association – for safer invalid cars. We've campaigned for years and still got nowhere. Come election time, everyone wants to jump on the bandwagon and champion the cause and promise action. Once an election is over, no one wants to know. Disabled people need all the mobility they can get – and safe mobility at that. God knows, they're handicapped enough as it is. It's so easy for the rest of us to overlook their needs. I doubt if I would have got interested or tried to do anything for them if I hadn't been disabled myself after the 1969 shunt when I injured my legs.

I was fortunate in that I was only temporarily disabled. I still haven't got full flexion in my legs and they are a lot weaker than they used to be, and still a bit bent. But I'm able to get around normally – whereas others can't. I do some exercises but I feel guilty I'm not doing more. I try to move quickly all the time and I take stairs two at a time rather than use the lifts. But, boy, am I lucky! It must be hell for those who can't. Disabled people have as much right as the rest of us to drive. Surely it's not asking too much to see that they are provided with cars that enable them to do so in safety. I hope the authorities will take notice and do something about them – not tomorrow, but right now!

I've always felt that if you're going to get the most out of life – you have to put yourself on the line. It may bring a lot of criticism, of course, but that's no bad thing if it enables you to see things that much clearer.

I was visiting a home for young cripples once and got talking to one of the lads who kept moaning about what a bloody awful place it was to live in. He was right, it was a bloody awful place; but if I agreed with him, he would probably have been there for the rest of his life. So I said: 'Well, what are you *doing* about it then?' He could have sworn at me, but he didn't. In fact, there was no need for him to say anything. His determined expression said it all.

One of the invitations Bette and I received in November was to go to Monte Carlo for a few days for the opening of the Hotel Loews. This presented a problem as Bette had a previous invitation to go to Hong Kong with Janet and Tony Brise as guests of Teddy Yip – everything paid. It was to be a holiday for the two girls and a holiday-cum-business trip for Tony, who had been invited there to watch the Macão Grand Prix and the Kart Grand Prix.

I was all set to go alone to Monte Carlo when Bette said, 'How about taking Brigitte?' This was a great idea and Bette rushed around like crazy to get her a new outfit for the occasion.

Bette and Janet had a super ten days in Hong Kong, with Tony joining them after five days; and Brigitte and I had an equally good three days in Monte Carlo. Brigitte is pretty good at French and that came in handy. It would have been nice to have taken Samantha with us as she is a little bundle of fun, but she was only ten.

When we got back home on Sunday, Bette had already flown in from Hong Kong. The three of us, and Samantha, obviously had a lot to say and that evening was going to be our only chance to talk as I was due at the team works first thing on Monday morning and there was a dinner to go to in London that evening.

We were busy getting the new car ready prior to testing and practice at the Paul Ricard circuit in the south of France later in the week. We had planned to race it in the first Grand Prix of the 1976 season which started in January, and here we were at the end of November so there wasn't all that much time to spare.

The National Sporting Club Dinner that night was being held in my honour but I had no idea who was going to be present. When I arrived at the Café Royal I was amazed to see so many of my friends there – and my father. Maybe they weren't feeding him too well at home!

As I stepped into the main reception room I was even more surprised to see my racing car; and I got a third surprise when I saw the menu. The cover had an illustration of my helmet decked out in my London Rowing Club racing colours with my name visible through a clear-view film visor.

There were 550 guests present and it was a very emotional moment. I felt choked though I hope I didn't show it. As I opened the menu I saw that David Benson, the

Motoring Editor of the *Daily Express*, had written a lengthy tribute to my career.

The food and wine were excellent and the company tremendous. The speakers proposing the toasts were formidable, too. When it came to my turn I had to speak after Eric Morecambe and Jackie Stewart. Following one comedian is difficult enough but imagine having to match the humour of two people like that.

Prince Rainier had been invited, but was unable to be present and my hosts presented me with a message from him. It was a beautiful inscription with one of the lines referring to my retirement in which he had written, 'Now we can grow old together.'

While I had been a racing driver I had often said to audiences during speeches and talks: 'You know the risks, you accept them. If man can't look at danger and still go on, man has stopped living. If the worst ever happens – then it means simply that I've been asked to pay the bill for the happiness of my life – without a moment's regret.'

17
by
Bette Hill

How could Graham know that he was not coming back after writing that last page . . . and yet it almost seems as though he did. I never knew he thought of me that way, but I realized the children and I were his anchor. It has made me even more proud to have been his wife and to know that I did make him happy.

On the Saturday evening of 29th November we were having a small dinner party with the couple who are our neighbours and old friends – Herb and Doreen Jones – and Fay Coakley, Brigitte's godmother who stays with us most week-ends and is a great comfort. It was a candle-lit dinner in the kitchen and I was expecting Graham back for lunch on Sunday – but he sent a telex message to say he would be back that Saturday night. They had finished testing at Paul Ricard and all the boys liked to get home and not hang about. It was about ten minutes to ten, I suppose, and we had just finished the dessert when the phone rang. It was a reporter from a Sunday newspaper and he asked: 'Is it true about Graham Hill?' I thought, 'Oh crikey – now what?' These people seldom know who they are talking to and often don't even ask. I thought he was after Graham for something trivial. I didn't really listen to what he was saying. So I simply put the receiver back. Before I could sit down again, Damon and Samantha rushed into the kitchen – with Damon looking white and

strained saying: 'Mummy – a plane has crashed in fog at
Arkley golf course on its way from Marseilles to Elstree. . . .
They think it's Daddy.'

Poor darling – he knew. He had been watching television – they hadn't mentioned any names – but instinc-
tively, he knew it had to be Graham.

I cannot remember too much of the next few hours
except that Dr Peter Turner and his wife Beryl, from the
house at the top of our drive, were in the hall. I had asked
them to come and join us for dinner that evening but
Peter was flat on his back in bed having damaged a disc.
But there he was – in his dressing gown. I asked what he
was doing there and told him he should be home in bed.
He had insisted on leaving his home, with Beryl, to see if
he could help. They looked so unhappy and I really
wondered why – it all seemed so unreal.

Larry and Margaret Webb were there, too. Herb Jones
had phoned Larry to come over and help and they had
come, despite the fog – as did so many people, and the
police. One of the policemen drove Fay to fetch Brigitte
from a party. Normally, I wouldn't have known the exact
address of her parties but that evening I asked her and
she had left the invitation on our bed. So there it was to
tell us where she could be found.

Fay and the policeman arrived at these unfortunate
people's home where their son was celebrating his twenty-
first birthday. They apologized for the intrusion and asked
for Brigitte. When she saw the policeman and auntie Fay
she said, quite calmly: 'It's Daddy, isn't it?'

The policeman said, 'Yes.'

When Brigitte asked if he was *sure*, and couldn't there
be a mistake – and he said 'No, there is no mistake,'
Brigitte fell apart and just screamed. Her young girl
friends in the room cried too, and the boys there were so
unhappy, and the poor mother and father were kind but a
trifle bewildered but doing all they could to pacify everyone . . . the party was over.

Shortly after I heard the news I had, apparently, taken
off down the drive. The strangest thing of all was that I

had run upstairs into our guest-room and put on my fur coat – then out of the front door and down the drive with Doreen Jones chasing after me. I was going where Graham was – and nothing was going to stop me.

Looking back, it was hysterical really – because there was poor Doreen trudging up the drive after me and she had a long skirt on, as I did, but I'd lifted mine up so as I could run hell for leather – and she was slowed down through leaving her skirt long and trying to be a little more ladylike than me.

She kept calling for me to stop – but I wouldn't listen, I was off . . . to be stopped by a police car coming towards me. The inspector (I think) got out and started to restrain me, together with Doreen. *Nothing* was going to stop me from going to Graham. I struggled but, after a wrestling match and banging on the roof of the panda car, I lost – and they finally got me back into the house. Doreen took a real beating. I hadn't realized I could be so strong.

The police told us later that there are three ways in which people react. They have the door shut in their faces . . . or the person faints . . . or they start beating the police. I'm obviously a violent number.

While this was going on Brigitte arrived home – distraught and pathetic. Graham's mother and father had also been fetched by the police and they arrived shocked and terribly sad.

That night was very confused and so are my recollections of it – but I remember the next one more clearly. Sian, who is Fay's daughter and also my god-daughter, came over with her father. She was seventeen and a great comfort to Brigitte who was a year younger – and she and a couple more of Brigitte's friends turned up, which was very sweet of them, so as they could all be with Brigitte and sleep in her room.

Samantha and Damon moved camp beds into my room to be with me. But before we went to bed everyone in the house stayed up to watch a tribute to Graham on the television. Connie, his mother, watched with us and and so did Cliff and Sylvia Davis. We all sat close to each

38. Golf became less frustrating after Henry Cooper and I took lessons from the maestro – John Jacobs.

39. Monte Carlo 1973. Breakfast with Stirling Moss – one of the greatest drivers the world has ever known.

40. Damon is a 'natural' trials rider and we practise together whenever we can around the grounds and woodlands of our home.

41. The Springfield Boys' Club is motor racing's boys' club and they get more out of life by putting more in.

42. Jackie Stewart visits the boys' club and Bette goes there whenever she can.

43. Bette and I get on well with Tony and Janet Brise. We all clicked the moment we met – which is great.

44. Bette

other – holding hands. Damon was at my feet and Samantha on my lap. When she shouted: 'Why did it have to be Daddy?' we all cried – even Cliff – and not one of us had a handkerchief. I asked Sian to go and get some Kleenex; she came back with a roll of toilet paper. We all laughed as she tore strips off for each of us. There was an awful lot of nose blowing!

So many people came to the house to comfort the children and me then and during the next few days. Eba Grant, Doreen and Les Leston, Liz Piper, Peter Jopp, Lynne Oliver, Peter and Ann Cameron-Webb, and Glenda Fox. Peggy Taylor flew over from her home in Nice; her boys and Damon had grown up together. Also, Sally Swart (Stokes) from Holland. Eddie and Penny Portman were on the phone constantly. They now have Graham's gun-dog Bel; and I have their youngest son as god-son, taking over from Graham.

During the next few days I felt I desperately needed someone to help me get in touch with all Graham's numerous friends and associates. So I immediately thought of Gabrielle White who had been Graham's secretary for some ten years. During that time she knew absolutely everyone and almost everything that Graham did and I had always kept in touch with her – and she was the very first person I thought of because of her ability and her closeness to us as a family.

I phoned her and, from the moment she arrived, she was the most incredible tower of strength – allowing herself only a few tears when she thought no one was watching – but I did know. She was able to assist everyone who didn't have telephone numbers at their finger-tips and she typed numerous letters for me.

One day her boss, Lister Welch who had been Graham's agent for ten years, came down with her. I asked him if he minded if I borrowed Gabrielle to help me out a while longer and he said, 'No – this is where she should be,' which I thought was incredibly kind. From that day on she has been just wonderful to me and whenever I get into a panic over various things she's the first one to say:

'Stop worrying – it's not that bad – we'll sort it out.'

Graham was so full of life. We had been married for twenty years. Even in all those years he was racing I always felt I would die before him. When he retired we were both very sad. I was sure even then that I'd be the first to go. How unkind life is. None of us, men and women friends of ours, could believe it and they still find it difficult to understand.

I never, ever, thought this would happen – he had such a charmed life, hadn't he? I never even thought he'd hurt himself very badly. When Colin Chapman phoned from America and said Graham had broken both legs – it felt as though he was talking about someone else, or that he was saying it was raining or the sun was shining. I just couldn't believe it could be Graham who'd died – not now, not after retiring.

A few days after Graham's funeral I was driving our gardener home. He's about seventy-two years of age – a lovely man. As I turned round to come back home I screamed out in the car: 'I don't believe this is happening to me.' I felt ill from keeping it all in, and then as I shouted out all alone in the car – suddenly, I felt light again.

Fay phoned when I got home and I told her about this. I said: 'You *have* to talk to yourself.' She said, 'I must try it.' That was sweet – but, honestly, if you talk it out with people who are suffering just as much as you are – one can share it . . . it gives a lot of comfort to each of you.

For some unknown reason, though, for about eight days, I felt as though I was in a trance. It was the strangest feeling. Then suddenly I woke one morning and it was gone. Almost as if – I had woken from a sleep. Whilst I was in this dream-like state I was doing things so automatically that I wasn't caring what I was doing. Nothing seemed to matter. But someone saw me who had gone through a similar situation – and she said that she could see it in my eyes. They were absolutely dead, and I was moving like a machine. However, that passed and I realized that I must pull myself together.

Graham always knew what to do. He was so strong. I always used to feel he was indestructible. I thought he was going to live till he was a hundred and it was so comforting because I believed I would never have to manage without him.

One thing I will never understand is why, after all these years of racing, he had to die in an air crash? I still find it unbelievable that I won't see him again.

Graham taught me to be strong. He had so much guts, dedication and love for his fellow men. He was a great example to us all. Thank God, because my children are going to need the strength. But they have taken it quite philosophically. I'm a trifle shattered. I'm no heroine. I'm only one of six women who lost their loved ones in the crash, and I'm not as brave as I look.

I have such a lot, my three fabulous children and the memories of being married to such an exciting and wonderful man for twenty years.

Everything was going so well. Graham had signed up with the sponsors. It really takes three years to get a team on its feet, and going. And that's what was happening.

Everybody had so much to live for. They were all beginning to give to the sport. Graham always gave – he hardly ever took. He gave of himself, his money, his time, everything. Tony Brise was about to do the same thing – to give a tremendous amount of pleasure to an enormous number of people. The car was going to be very competitive and we all had tremendous high hopes.

I also thought we had another couple like Jackie Stewart and Helen on our hands. Glamorous people again. Janet was very photogenic – she had been a model. And I thought – here we go again – lots of glamorous photographs in amongst motor racing.

Graham was forty-six – Tony was exactly half his age. The Team were all so young. Andy Smallman was twenty-four, Terry Richards twenty-six, Ray Brimble thirty-four, and Tony Alcock thirty-five.

I know Janet – but I don't know the other wives too well. I've met Pat Brimble twice. I met Terry Richards' wife, Linda, at race meetings at Brands and Silverstone and often had a cup of tea together in the Revcon. Andy the designer, wasn't married. Tony Alcock had only just joined the team. I've since met his wife, Kathleen, and she was expecting a baby. She had a son whom she named Anthony Jason – the second name being that of their first son who was drowned in Australia. Kathleen has so much courage – as they *all* have.

Janet and I have been very close. When we went to Hong Kong together and Tony met us out there he was very happy that we got on so well together. The crash knocked her for six – it knocked us all for six. She came here one day during the week of the funerals with her parents. She is the only child – and they were marvellous. Her parents are very good and strong. When she arrived here she looked just like one other girl I had seen in motor racing who had lost her fiancé. Complete emptiness in her face. And I'd been surrounded by people who were all sort of cosseting me and doing things for me – and I know her parents were doing an awful lot for her, too. When she came to me – I thought: 'Oh my God. What have I done?' and from that moment on we were very good for each other. I helped her over the ghastly bits – we both cried together, and we both laughed together.

Her father said to me, as she left for their Birmingham home: 'She hadn't eaten until she came here.' We had sat down with about twenty-three people, all friends. The girls were doing the cooking. Gabrielle was answering the phone and the men were making plans and arranging everything for the next week or so. Janet was able to talk and as we talked she visibly came alive again. As she left – her eyes were brighter and her face had colour – and she said: 'You've done wonders for me.' I hoped I had.

Graham's funeral was held at St Albans Abbey. I really don't remember much about what my own feelings were. I was able to think about the questions I was asked as to the arranging of the funeral – and the flowers I wanted to send – but everything seemed terribly numb. People do behave differently. Some cry, others look so lost for words though obviously they feel terribly sorry. I needed their pity because it helped. But I didn't want people to sob all over me – and I wasn't going to sob all over them. I cried on my own and with the children and family. If I hadn't I would probably have been ill.

During the drive from the house through the country the police provided motor cycle outriders for the procession of four Daimlers. Near St Albans, police cars took over. The traffic was stopped at every roundabout along the route to let us straight through, and all the policemen on duty saluted. When we arrived at St Albans the streets were lined – and the police and traffic wardens there saluted too. It really was most impressive.

All the men – John Coombs, Herb Jones, Larry Webb, Jackie Stewart, Peter Jopp, Les Leston (and if I've missed out any forgive me) had arranged the funeral service – and they very much wanted to be pall-bearers. Then there were lots of cousins and close friends who wanted to be ushers. So they were, together with Lord Portman, Henry Cooper, Eric Morecambe, Charles Benson, Denny Hulme, Peter Gethin, Innes Ireland, Jimmy Hill and David Benson. That's how it worked out. They were comforting for the people as they arrived in the Abbey.

Graham's mother and father were there, of course – and Janet Brise. Emerson Fittipaldi, James Hunt, Tim Schenken, John Surtees, Roy Salvadori, Ronnie Peterson, Howden Ganley, Rolf Stommelen, Prince Metternich, Lord Snowdon, Lord Brabourne, Lord Montagu, Sir Clive Bossom, Tommy Sopwith, Harry Hyams – and many more of our friends and their wives, but it's impossible to list them all. There were so many people inside and outside the Abbey. I remember there being crowds but I don't remember any faces.

The Bishop of St Albans – the Rt. Rev. Robert Runcie – had come to me just before the funeral and asked me to choose the Hymns. I chose 'Jerusalem' because Graham loved it. Also because it was one of the hymns that was sung at Piers Courage's funeral – I had looked out of

Piers' church window and seen England as Graham loved England, and as Piers loved England, and it seemed just right for both of them – particularly with those fabulous last two lines:

> Till we have built Jerusalem
> In England's green and pleasant land

The children and I arrived at the Abbey with Graham's parents, and his auntie Gladys, and Fay; for absolutely no reason at all, when I got inside the Abbey and saw the Dean in his robes – I kissed him! Don't ask me why: his was a familiar kind face smiling at me, so I kissed him. A few days later I was so embarrassed. I hope he understood.

It was a beautiful service. Samantha stood in awe of the whole service not really knowing what was going on, except that she did say afterwards: 'Oh Mummy, I was very worried about those men holding Daddy. They didn't look very steady.' She was referring of course, to the pall-bearers which brought on a giggle from one or two of us.

Brigitte's an adorable creature – with an awful lot of Graham in her. She chose 'There is a green hill far away' as the other hymn. There were twelve of her girl friends from her school sitting in the Abbey behind where the choir were. They were all in their blue and yellow striped blazers. They were watching her obviously. Each one had met Graham at some time or another, and as they were all pretty attractive young creatures he took a great fancy to them and chatted them up in his inimitable way. Having seen them sitting there she said: 'I'm not going to cry, I'm not going to cry.' And of course the moment 'There is a green hill far away' started – she couldn't stop. She was sobbing and she said: 'Oh, * * * *!' She told me afterwards and said: 'Oh Mummy, I swore.'

Damon's friends came too: six smartly dressed young boys looking older than their years had come out of respect for Graham and fondness for Damon. Graham had taken them to various races and also given them a flip in the aeroplane. He was a man's man and was always able to treat young and old alike.

Graham used to say that if there's a life hereafter – he would consider it being a bit of a bonus. If he does know what's going on down here . . . I bet he had a chuckle at the things that happened at his funeral.

There were 3000 people inside, and another 1000 outside who listened to the service through loudspeakers. Graham was there in spirit at the Abbey. There were disabled people in wheelchairs in the aisles – and a man in an iron-lung in the vestry – listening to the ceremony. Unbelievable! There were twenty-four boys from the Springfield Boys' Club, too.

John Coombs read the lesson, beautifully. The Bishop was simply marvellous – considering he'd only met Graham a few times and that was at the Abbey and he didn't really have a long conversation with him. He briefed himself with the help of one or two friends – but came out with just the right summing up. In his Address he said: 'Graham brought happiness to millions. Whether you knew him from a distance, or close to, he was *for real.*'

There were lots of sniffles in the Abbey, I could hear them going on, but I just could not cry. Nothing would come. I had to hand Damon a handkerchief because he had a little weep. When I walked up the aisle, after the service, with Damon clutching my hand – I saw a girl friend sobbing her heart out. It hurt me to see her so upset. I just grabbed her arm and called her name.

The family and I went with the cortège to Garston Crematorium for a private cremation and then came home.

When we arrived back at the house I was staggered at the number of cars in the drive. We had said to people, 'Do come back and have a drink and a little bit of something to eat,' because I feel that people need something to soften the blow after a funeral. And it was good to see them anyway. I loved them coming back though I think I went through that in a daze – I often ask now was so and so at the funeral? And did so and so come back to the house? And my friends say, 'Oh, yes – they were here.'

That evening we even laughed – through some kind of false gaiety. Looking back I can't think why . . . reaction I suppose.

One of the incredible things that happened was that at Tony's funeral, which was the day before Graham's, Janet had chosen the same hymn 'Jerusalem'. The other hymn she had chosen was 'Morning is broken' – the lovely Cat Stevens song. That threw me a bit. Jackie Stewart was standing with me, and a friend called David Haines – they were very kind. They had driven me to the funeral in Kent. The moment I heard the music, I choked. Jackie folded up the paper with the words of the hymn on it. I immediately pushed it open – took a deep breath – and sung at the top of my voice – because that was the only way I could keep going. If I had allowed myself to cry I would never have been able to pull myself together again that day so I said, 'Sing – we've got to sing' . . . and we did.

A week after the accident I had to say to myself, 'The children must go back to school. We've got to start again. Monday is the beginning of the week – we start on Monday. Everybody in the house has got to go. Everybody that would not normally be here must leave.'

My parents-in-law went back home. Cruel, perhaps – but I decided on that Monday morning that we all had to start doing our own thing. I pulled Brigitte out of bed and she said, 'I don't want to go to school.'

'Darling, you *have* to go,' I said, 'today is Monday and we have to start from the beginning of the week. Tomorrow, it will be even more difficult. So up you get, come on.' We had a cuddle and a cry – and I said, 'Come on darling.' So I took Brigitte and Samantha to school that morning.

The person I felt most sorry for was poor old Damon because he and Graham were like *ONE*. They had the motor-bike trials and things which they used to do. Graham discussed the cars, the plane, and the bikes with Damon – shooting too – as though he was a younger brother. They used to ride their motor-bikes around the woods in the grounds together.

If Damon knows I'm feeling low, he's always there. He's only fifteen. A long time ago he said: 'I'm fed up with women.' I told him I didn't blame him. There was grandma, a nanny, his two sisters, me, and auntie Fay. Damon so loved being with Graham – and Graham so enjoyed being with him. At that age, you see, they were getting much closer. It's a darn shame, isn't it!

I have a fabulous photograph of Graham in my bedroom – taken by Helen Stewart. It gives me terrific strength. I talk to Graham now and again – I hate that sort of thing really, anything uncanny, but sometimes I feel that he is still talking to me. Obviously, I have good days and bad days. But I walk past his picture and if things are a bit tough I say: 'How am I doing?' And I can feel him say: 'Mmmm – not bad.' But sometimes I say: 'I need your strength today.'

There are so many pictures of Graham about the house; pictures of him and the children laughing and playing. He used to say: 'Why do you have all those pictures out?' – and I said, 'Because I like them.'

People sometimes think they'll hurt me if they talk about Graham. They won't. I always adored talking about him when he was alive. I'll never stop talking about him. He's still terribly alive to me but I miss being able to put my arms around him.

However – to return to that fabulous picture. When I went up to my bedroom on Christmas Eve it was gone and I couldn't find it anywhere. I had taken Damon down to the shops earlier – he'd been very secretive about what he was doing. Then I thought – *that's who has it.*

On Christmas morning which, of course, we were all dreading – but which went off quite well and very happily as Graham would have wanted it – I left Damon's present on the Christmas tree until last because I knew what it was going to be and I knew it would throw me. When I opened it up it was just as I thought. Damon had taken the picture down to the shop and had it framed for me – it *did* throw me. I didn't cry there and then – I went upstairs. Brigitte came up after me, and when she saw me

I told her I didn't mean to cry but I couldn't help it. She said, 'Oh Mummy – of course you cry if you want to.'

Janet Brise came for a week-end in the middle of January. She went to Scotland before Christmas, then spent Christmas at her parent's home in Birmingham. She had to face going back to her own house in Kent, some time or other. She hadn't been back there for virtually six weeks so it was very tough. I told her, 'Come on, you've go to do it, you can't keep putting it off,' and she said, 'I know, I know.' So she decided to go home on the Monday after spending the week-end with us. I suggested she should go somewhere first – as she had a girl friend coming to stay with her who wouldn't be there until after work that day. So she went to Tony's parents.

Tony's mother had been over to Janet's home and put some flowers in to brighten the rooms. I knew that she would – she's that sort of person. Janet had lunch with Tony's parents and stayed there until her girl friend arrived back from work – then the two of them went to Janet's home together. There were masses of letters waiting for her, and photographs that people had sent, but it was hard for her.

Afterwards she said to me, 'It's not so bad, you know. I'm glad you said you can't keep putting it off.' So that's the way it is – the more you put it off, the more difficult it becomes.

I sometimes *try* to pray. At the moment I find it very difficult to even believe that someone, somewhere, could take Graham from me.

When Jackie Stewart was driving me down to Ray Brimble's funeral (he had already driven me to Tony Brise's funeral the day before Graham's) . . . I don't know why I asked him this – but I just said: 'Do you pray?' and he said 'Yes.' When I was at Andy Smallman's funeral at Golders Green I asked Peter Jopp (whose small son is my god-son) if he prayed? And he said, 'Oh yes, often. . . . When we heard of the accident we were all terribly upset – we actually got down on our knees and said a prayer for you and the children.'

These are men that I would never have thought would pray. So, in a way, it makes me think that there must be someone – some divine power taking us to what Father Easty (the American padre at Watkins Glen) said is 'a far better place'. But it still does not explain to me why, if Graham was to die, did five other young people have to go with him?

Brigitte and I were only confirmed two years ago. Graham would never take communion if I was with him because he would not leave me sitting alone in a pew. So when Brigitte said she wanted to be confirmed, I joined her. I think that is why I find it hard to believe 100 per cent.

Graham crashed in fog at night into trees at Arkley golf course while approaching his home base at Elstree which was only three miles away. At first, of course, they wouldn't let me go out there. I wanted to go to Graham and I kept saying, 'Can't I go and see him?' But they said, 'No, no, no – you can't.' All I wanted to do was put my arms round him once more.

I told Herb Jones, 'I must go out to the crash – I want to see it, because those newspaper pictures are awful. Those black and white pictures with policemen sifting through all that stuff . . . I know it's not like that and I want to see it.'

A girl friend said: 'You must do as you want. If you want to go . . . go.' So Herb Jones fixed it up with the golf club and with the police so that there wouldn't be any sightseers.

I said to Damon: 'Darling, I'm going up to see where Daddy crashed. Do you want to come with me?'

He said positively, 'No.'

Herb, Doreen, and I started to go out of the house. As we did so – Damon shouted: 'Wait – I'm coming with you.' He put on his Embassy jacket and came out with us.

It was a lovely, bright morning – and I'm *so* glad I went!

I'm sorry now I didn't go closer than I did. Because it

wasn't awful like the pictures showed in the papers. It was peaceful, it was beautiful, there were some lovely trees and a copse. I didn't go right up to it that day. I said, 'I'm so glad.'

Damon was a bit frightened of course. I was too, and I'm sure the other two were petrified of what was going to happen – I suppose they thought I'd go berserk, but I didn't.

As for Damon – I think it helped him quite a bit too. He discussed it with Herb and the police inspector and said: 'Oh, they must have come in from there – and he must have been doing a circuit that way . . . then they came in there, there and there.' The three men discussed how, why, and what happened.

When we came back – once again, it was like shouting to myself in the car. I felt a great weight had lifted.

Later on I told Janet what I had done . . . and another time I told Fay, who loved Graham dearly: 'I'd like to go out,' she said, 'and put some daffodils or something like that there.'

So one day we went to the nursery and bought some daffodil bulbs, and a pot of chrysanthemums as I wanted to put some colour there. Fay and I went to the golf course and tip-toed along like a couple of criminals. I said, 'Gosh, if Graham were to see us now he'd say, "You stupid twits – what *are* you doing?"'

We went up to the trees – that was really not too nice because one particular tree was pretty charred and the roots had been, literally, forced out of the ground – but it wasn't horrible. Fay started to cry. She said, 'Now I know he's dead.' I said gently: 'Oh for God's sake. I brought you for some support. Don't start crying now.'

We put the pot of chrysanths in the earth – then we started to plant the daffodil bulbs. We giggled nervously. Fay said, 'Which way up do you put them?' Poor girl, she was so confused. I said: 'Oh goodness. Look – these are the roots, these are the roots. That's the way they go in the ground.' And we shoved them in.

While we were doing this – over on the green, just a few yards away – there were some golfers trying not to notice us. Anyway, we just had a little look around and we walked away. It was most comforting.

I've been there several times since. I asked the captain of the golf club if it embarrassed the members – he said it didn't. If I'm feeling low, and want to be near Graham, I go over to that copse. I feel so close to him and the other boys when I'm there. I really do. You must think I'm out of my mind – but I'm not. I just chat to them – and it's wonderful.

Janet wants to go there, too. But it was still winter – and I wanted her to go when it was a bit more spring-like.

I shall continue to go to motor races – and I hope that I will keep up with the Grands Prix. It was so much part of our lives that – to not go, I think, would leave a tremendous void. The thing is . . . they weren't killed racing!

I have been to Brands Hatch for the Race of Champions. I went there, almost, as a dress rehearsal for myself to meet all the drivers and the mechanics again. I was afraid I might embarrass them – but they were so welcoming and warm.

An Italian mechanic working on Niki Lauda's car looked up sideways to me and clasped my hand. It was so spontaneous it nearly made me cry.

Eba Grant is always around at these times. She is secretary to the Doghouse Club which is run to raise money for charities by the wives and girl friends of people connected with motor racing. She always manages to pick people up from the shattered pieces – and, apart from being Samantha's god-mother, she is a truly kind and wonderful friend.

I have also been to Silverstone, of course, for the Graham Hill International Trophy Race. This was quite an incredible day. I would never have thought I was capable of doing what I did. I rushed around almost as though Graham was still there working on his cars and even driving. I said 'Hello' to all the people I knew. I was very busy, I never seemed to stop. I know that Graham would have loved this day. On the practice day I was presented with his retirement present – and on the race day, of course, James Hunt won and I presented him with the Graham Hill Trophy. He would have been very proud, and very happy and, I believe, happy for me too. There were some ups and downs on that day. My mood was very high and low but, overall, I have to say that there is no way that I could detach myself from the scene. I have many warm and wonderful friends in the motor racing world.

There is one thing which is even more strange. On the BBC *Keepsakes* programme – Graham took with him an address book which I gave him in 1954. He tells you about it in one of the earlier chapters. I put in it: 'To you my darling – lest you forget.' This was before we were married. 'All my Love, Bette 1954.' We were married in 1955.

He wouldn't part with that book. Apart from the fact that it was full of addresses it had lots of punch lines of various jokes. It was absolutely falling apart – it was sellotaped everywhere. If he was ever lost for a joke he would produce this book and be able to tell one. Eventually he had to transfer them into the back of his new diaries – but still kept this one with him.

This address book was found at the accident. The top half of his briefcase was thrown clear with the address book in it amongst his papers which I find strange . . . *it had come back to me after all these years.*

Graham now lies in the graveyard of the fourteenth-century church of St Boltoph's in our village of Shenley. His grave is against a beautiful flintstone wall. Just beside him are six children – aged between a few days, one month, and two years, and Joannie who was eleven years old. The Pied Piper had returned to the little children he always enjoyed being with.

One mother wrote to me and said: 'It makes me strangely happy to have my little one lying next to this good and wonderful man.'

The stone I have put there is inscribed:

Death hides it does not divide,
Thou art on Christ's side,
Thou with Christ and Christ with me,
So together still are we.

Tragedy is a test of courage – if you can live up to it, it will make you a better person than when it first met you. I often feel I just cannot go on. I get this dreadful empty feeling . . . it doesn't get any better. Then there is a cry from Samantha asking if I know where her so-and-so is, or I hear Brigitte singing whilst practising for the lead in the *Pirates of Penzance*. And in the evening, as I sit in Graham's study I can hear from Damon's room above the rather tuneless strumming of his guitar. I realize then that I have to go on with it all – even if the 'missing' never ends.

Samantha says, 'I used to love the big parties we had here.'

She shall have her big parties – though they may not be as big or as lovely – but she shall have them. The children that Graham and I had shall have what it is humanly possible for them to have *and* the good life he planned for them.